JEWISH

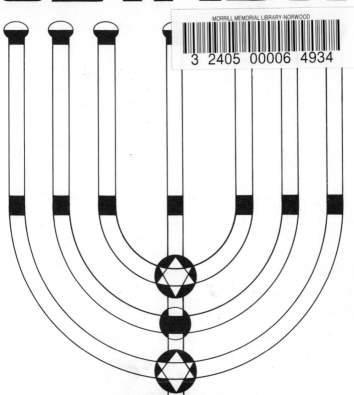

TRIVIA

JANE LENARSKY
DODE B. LEVENSON
BARBARA WACHMAN

Copyright © 1985 by
Quinlan Press, Inc.
All rights reserved
including the right of reproduction
in whole or in part in any form
Published by Quinlan Press, Inc.
131 Beverly Street
Boston, MA 02114
(617) 227-4870
1-800-551-2500

Cover Design by Joan McLaughlin

Library of Congress Catalog Card Number
84-63112
ISBN 0-9611268-7-6
Photo Credits:
Israeli Consulate of New York City
Newport R.I. Historic Association
Joshua Seth Wachman

First printing April 1985
Second printing May 1985
Third printing October 1985

"He kisseth the lips that giveth the right answer."

Proverbs 24:26

Barbara Wachman was born a bibliophile in NYC. She received an M.Ed. in special education from Boston University in 1965. A teacher by profession, and wife and mother by choice, she lives in a suburb west of Boston with her husband and children.

Although there is nothing trivial about **Jane Lenarsky**, she was born and raised in NYC. Having attended Russell Sage College and Boston University, she holds an M.Ed. in guidance & counseling, and a C.A.G.S. in school psychology. She is presently working as a school adjustment counselor and living in a suburb of Boston. She and Barbara Wachman are first cousins.

Dode B. Levenson was raised under the proper and watchful eye of his mother Marlyn and his father, Rabbi Paul Levenson, in Prairie Village, Kansas. In addition to being a full-time Jew, Dode has found time to attend the University of Massachusetts in Amherst and become editor-in-chief of the Massachusetts Daily *Collegian,* president of the Communications Club and editor-in-chief of *Intercom,* the undergraduate communications newsletter.

Table of Contents

QUESTIONS

HISTORY AND POLITICS

1. In what month and what year did Israel gain its independence?

2. The first kosher butcher on the American continent was also a *shochet* (ritual slaughterer). Who was he?

3. Name the man who succeeded F.D. Roosevelt as governor of New York.

4. Who was the English-born Jew who founded and served as the first president of the American Federation of Labor?

5. In what year was Brandeis University opened?

6. Who was the British soldier, known as "Lawrence of Judea," who trained men of the Haganah to protect the Iraq-Haifa oil pipeline in 1936?

7. What was the name of the first high commissioner to Palestine under the British Mandate?

8. Name the Connecticut politician who served as governor, congressman, Secretary of H.E.W. and senator.

9. Who is the former ambassador to England who is also the publisher of the *Philadelphia Inquirer, TV Guide, Seventeen* and *The Daily Racing Form?*

10. By what other name was the Earl of Beaconsfield known?

11. Who was the Soviet Jewish statesman who served as the Kremlin's emissary to the U.S. in 1933?

12. Michael Dukakis, two time Governor of Massachusetts is married to the daughter of a Jewish musician who is the associate director of the Boston Pops. Name him.

13. Who is known as the first Jew to die in the American Revolution?

14. What was the name of the college on whose grounds Brandeis University was established?

15. Name the man who is reported to have contributed more to the cause of the American Revolution than any other Jewish civilian or soldier.

16. Which president of the United States appointed the first Jew (Mordecai Noah) to a high diplomatic post in the U.S. foreign service?

17. Who was president of Israel when that country celebrated its 25th anniversary?

18. Which U.S. president appointed Oscar Straus Secretary of Commerce, rendering him the first Jew to hold a Cabinet office?

19. A newspaper, published in Boston since 1903, was for a time regarded as the most influential English language newspaper on Jewish topics. What is its name?

20. Name the labor leader who was advisor to Eleanor and F.D. Roosevelt and was president of the I.L.G.W.U. from 1932-1966.

21. Who ruled Egypt when that country fought against Israel in 1948?

22. Which U.S. president appointed Henry Morgenthau Sr. ambassador to Turkey?

23. Herman Bernstein, journalist, novelist and playwright, founded which Yiddish newspaper in 1914?

24. In 1922 a Jew was appointed president of the General Electric Company. What was his name?

25. Gerard Swope's brother was a prominent journalist. What was his name, and what was his most important post as journalist?

26. Name the one-time Harvard Law Professor who defended Sacco and Venzetti.

27. Name the rabbi, physician, and philosopher who was called on to heal King Richard I of England.

28. What Dutch-born Jewish philosopher was the author of *Ethics* (1677)?

29. Who succeeded Menachem Begin as prime minister of Israel?

30. The inscription on the Liberty Bell in Philadelphia, "Proclaim liberty throughout all the land unto all the inhabitants thereof," is a quote from what book?

31. Who is the person who served longest as mayor of modern Jerusalem?

32. Name five Jews who served on the U.S. Supreme Court.

33. Name the person to whom Lord Balfour addressed his famous declaration.

34. Who was the hero in the war of 1812 who was instrumental in abolishing flogging in the U.S Navy?

35. General U.S. Grant issued General Order No. 11 in 1862. Later, Abraham Lincoln revoked it. What was this order?

36. An English Jew of Portugese ancestry was elected to the General Assembly of South Carolina in 1774. Who was he?

37. Who was the only Jewish viceroy of India?

38. Who was the Egyptian ruler during the Six Day War of 1967?

39. Who was the philanthropist that aided Clara Barton in the founding of the American Red Cross?

40. The first Monday in September was set as a legal holiday to honor the American Labor Movement. Who was most instrumental in persuading Congress to do this?

41. What tragic event occurred between Monday, June 5 and Saturday, June 11?

42. Which U.S. colonel resigned his post to join the newly formed Israeli Army and was then killed by mistake by one of his own sentries during the Israeli War for Independence?

43. Which Jewish politician served twice as lord mayor of Dublin?

44. Who was president of the United States on the day the government recognized and welcomed the new state of Israel into the family of nations?

45. What gift did Chaim Weizmann present to President Harry Truman?

46. In dedicating the Bunker Hill monument in Charlestown, Massachusetts (1843), Daniel Webster referred to two benefactors, "Christian and Jew," who made the project possible. Who were they?

47. Where, in 1903, did the British statesman Joseph Chamberlain propose to found a Jewish state?

48. Baron Maurice de Hirsch proposed to finance major emigration of Russian Jews to which South American country?

49. The oldest Jewish cemetery in the New World was consecrated in 1659. Where is it?

50. Which is the only New England town with a permanent Jewish settlement since before the Revolution?

51. The Hasidic movement was opposed by a faction known as the Mitnaggedim. Who was the first leader of this faction (18th century)?

52. In order for Arthur J. Goldberg to accept the appointment as American ambassador to the UN, he had to resign what position?

53. Name the Argentine Jewish journalist who suffered under the Junta and recorded his ordeal in a widely read book *Prisoner Without a Name, Cell Without a Number*.

54. Who was the king that destroyed the first temple?

55. Which Jewish woman lawyer served three terms as a member of the U.S. House of Representatives? (She loved hats.)

56. A trend of thought in American Jewish life called Reconstructionism was originated in 1934 by whom?

57. The oldest Italian Jewish family traces its roots to Rome before Titus. What was their name?

58. What European emperor decreed (1809) that all Jews in his empire assume family names?

59. The minister of NYC Congregation Shearith Israel was one of 13 clergymen invited to the inauguration of George Washington. Who was he?

60. Under the rule of King Ferdinand of Spain, the Jews were either to convert or leave. What year were they expelled?

61. Which former Israeli ambassador to the UN hosted a TV documentary on Jewish heritage and civilization?

62. Name the Jew who helped in the Italian struggle for independence from Austria and was elected in 1877 to the Italian Senate.

63. Whom did Jacob Javits of New York succeed in the U.S. Sentate?

64. Name the Jewish journalist who, as a member of the staff of the *Washington Post* was instrumental in exposing a scandal involving *All The President's Men.*

65. Name the seven prime ministers of Israel (1948-1984).

66. "His Majesty's Government view with favour the establishment in Palestine of a national home for the Jewish people...." This is a portion of a letter known by what name?

67. Which Israeli politician was known as the father of Israel's foreign service and architect of its international diplomacy?

68. How many years is the president of Israel's term of office?

69. The first Jew to be elected to the U.S. Senate represented Louisiana and was later appointed secretary of state to the Confederacy. Who was he?

70. Where and when was the first edition of the *Jerusalem Talmud* printed?

71. Which former Israeli paratrooper became the first *sabra* ambassador to the UN?

72. In 1970 a Jewish politician was elected governor of Pennsylvania. Who was he?

73. By what name was the British government statement on restriction of Jewish immigration to Palestine (1939) known?

74. Leopold Karpeles won the Congressional Medal of Honor, quite a distinction for a Jew at that time. Which president bestowed it upon him?

75. Name the first liberal arts college for women under Jewish auspices in the United States. It opened in 1954.

76. What is the name of the Jewish premier of France who urged the French people to give up wine and drink milk?

77. Identify the president of Israel who once headed the biophysics section of the Weizmann Institute.

78. The first president of Brandeis University was Abram L. Sachar. Name the two presidents that succeeded him.

79. Who was the first *sabra* prime minister of Israel?

80. In which war did groups of American women knit hats for Israeli soldiers?

81. Who was the first Jewish mayor of New York City?

82. Which president of Israel was born in Ireland, educated at Cambridge, England and was a political commentator on the BBC?

83. Name Israel's first ambassador to Canada who also served as ambassador to the UN and the Court of St. James.

84. He was a brilliant orator and writer who organized the Red Army in the Russian Revolution. Who was he?

85. How many members are elected to the Israeli Knesset?

86. Bar Kochba's revolt marked the last period of Jewish independence and statehood until modern times. When was this revolt?

87. Which two heads of former enemy states won the Nobel Peace Prize in 1978?

88. Theodor Herzl wrote *Judenstaat* (which served as the seed of modern Zionism) after covering a notorious French trial as a journalist. Who was on trial?

89. Since 1652, heads of state, influential merchants and others proposed sites for Jewish colonies. Name the head of state who offered Ben-Gurion such a site in 1946.

90. Approximately how many Jews were there in America at the outset of the Revolution?

91. Who was the first Jew to take a seat on the judicial branch of Great Britain?

92. What post did these people hold in common: Theodor Herzl, David Wolff-sohn, Otto Warburg, Chaim Weizmann, Nahum Sokolow, Nahum Goldmann?

93. Name the first Jewish hospital established in the U.S.

94. The first U.S. college to train men for the Reform Movement Rabbinate was established in 1875 in Cincinnati, Ohio. What is its name?

95. Where was the first Sphardi synagogue on the Western hemisphere established?

96. Who became the first governor of Georgia?

97. Who was the first Jew to serve in the U.S. Senate?

98. Who was the first Jew to win all rights and privileges as a citizen of the New World?

99. The first Jewish settler in the U.S. came from Holland (1654) on a ship called the *Peartree*. Name him.

100. The first Jew to earn a college degree in North America graduated from Harvard, where he taught Hebrew for 40 years using a grammar text which he wrote. Who was he?

101. Name the first Jewish associate justice of the U.S. Supreme Court.

102. Name all of Israel's presidents to 1985.

103. The blockade of what passage in the Gulf of Elath prompted the 1956 Arab-Israeli War?

104. On March 27, 1979 a peace treaty was signed between Egypt and Israel.

Name the three men who signed the document.

105. "I will give you the law in one sentence: whatever is hateful to you, do not do to your neighbor. The rest of the laws are commentary." Who made this statement?

106. What university is named for a Supreme Court justice who was appointed by President Wilson in 1916?

107. The Marranos were faced with exile or death unless they converted to Christianity. In which countries was this decreed?

108. Rabbi Harold Friedman served his congregation in North Carolina in a mobile synagogue. What name was given to this mobile unit?

109. What does *Haskalah* refer to?

110. Who was the first Jew to graduate from West Point?

111. Before he founded the Hasidic movement, he was a Melamed, a ritual slaughterer and a lime burner. What was his name?

112. Luis de Torres, a Spanish Jew, was an interpreter for which explorer?

113. Who was the first Jewish chaplain in the U.S. Army?

114. In 1984-1985, the Israeli government was involved in a mission they referred to as "Operation Moses." What was this mission?

115. She was a teacher in Baltimore before she founded Hadassah. Who was she?

116. Jacob Lumbrozo was the first Jew in America to practice a profession which every Jewish mother wants for her son. What was his profession?

117. Who was the statesman that was the grandfather of Barbara Tuchman, the U.S. writer?

118. Who made an abortive attempt (1825) to establish a colony for European Jews on Grant Island, New York, in the Niagara River? What was the colony to be called?

119. Who was the first Jewish Miss America and in what year did she win her title?

120. After the death of Chaim Weizmann, which international figure was offered and declined the post of President of Israel?

121. What is the name of the British general who is credited with "liberating" Palestine from the Turks in WWI?

122. Who was the Jewish engineer who donated his library to the city of San Francisco and also served as mayor of that city (1894)?

123. By what Roman name is the historian Yosef-Ben-Matityahu known?

124. Yigael Yadin, the archaeologist, uncovered the history of what important site?

125. In 1968 this *sabra* military commander was appointed deputy prime minister of Israel. In addition, he was minister of education and culture. Who is he?

126. In the 1960's these two young Jewish radicals advocated distrust of anyone over the age of 30. They have lived to outgrow those ideas. Who were they?

127. Who is known as the "Father of the Reform Movement" in the U.S.? He founded the Union of American Hebrew Congregations.

128. Name the first Israeli woman to win the title Miss Universe.

129. Who was the first women to be ordained a Rabbi in the U.S.?

130. Name the English philanthropist who served the Rothschilds and was the first Jew in modern times to be knighted.

131. This husband and wife team serve in the same *schul*. Stuart Gertman is the rabbi; what position does his wife, Sarah Sager, hold?

132. Ludwig Zamenhof created an international language to promote international understanding. Name that language.

133. What was Zamenhof's profession?

134. Name the former Israeli defense minister who sued *Time* Magazine for libel.

135. Who was who? Match the names.

1. Lev Davidovich Bronstein	A. Zalman Shazar
2. Aubrey Even	B. Shimon Peres
3. David Green (Gruen)	C. Izhak Ben-Zvi
4. Ephraim Katchalsky	D. Leon Trotsky
5. Shimon Persky	E. Moshe Sharett
6. Izhak Shimshelevich	F. Abba Eban
7. Moshe Shertok	G. Ephraim Katzir
8. Zalman Rubashov	H. Levi Eshkol
9. Levi Shkolnik	I. David Ben Gurion

GOOD SPORTS

1. Why did Sandy Koufax, pitcher for the Dodgers, miss a game of the 1965 World Series?

2. The 1984 New Jersey Jr. Welterweight champ is known as "Zion The Lion." What is his real name?

3. She was the Professional Rookie of the Year in 1975-76. Name this golfer.

4. Nat Fleischer developed the ranking System used in what sport today?

5. His teammates said about this catcher: "He spoke seven languages but couldn't hit a curve ball in any of them." A lawyer and "Information Please" guest, who was he?

6. The "hitless" catcher mentioned above eventually served the U.S. government. In what capacity did he serve?

7. Mona Karff and Gisela Gresser are international masters in what game?

8. What position did Albert "Dolly" Stark hold in major league baseball?

9. Name the quarterback and referee in the N.F.L. who was also a congressman from Pennsylvania.

10. Which baseball team was owned by Julius and Max Fleischmann?

11. Name the basketball star who played with the original Celtics, coached at C.C.N.Y. and helped establish basketball in Israel.

12. Angelica Rosenau, who left Rumania for Israel, held 17 world titles in what sport?

13. Who is the former pitcher known as "The Clown Prince of Baseball?"

14. In what event in the 1948 and 1952 Olympics did Henry Wittenberg win gold and silver medals?

15. Carroll Rosenbloom was owner of the L.A. Rams. What other team did he once own?

16. Who was M.V.P. and Rookie of the Year in the International League in 1965?

17. Name the coach who lead his team to fifteen N.B.A. titles.

18. A leading proponent of women's pro tennis, this woman published and edited *World Tennis*. What is her name?

19. Who is sometimes referred to as "The Father of the World Series"?

20. Known as "The Mouth" because of his manner of reporting the sports news, this sports writer changed his last name from Cohen. By what name do we know him?

21. With what sport was the Viennese Hakoah Club associated in the 1920's?

22. Daniel Mendozo, who was the first Jew to win a title in this sport, has been referred to as the "Father of Scientific _____"?

23. He played with the Phillies (circa 1914-15) and was known as "Scissors." Name him.

24. Which football player was a Columbia U. halfback, a College Hall of Famer, Pro Hall of Famer and quarterback for the Chicago Bears (1940)?

25. Who won the major league batting crown in 1935?

26. Name the world chess champion, son of a cantor, who held the title from 1894 until he was defeated by Capablanca in 1921.

27. What is the name of the games approved by the International Olympic Committee which are held every four years in Israel?

28. What basketball team was founded by Abe Saperstein?

29. Two Jewish players made the American Davis Cup team in 1951. Who were they?

30. This convert to Judaism was an infielder with the Minnesota Twins and L.A. Angels and a six time A.L. batting champ. What is his name?

31. In what sport did Vic Hershkowitz win 30 national championships?

32. Barnet Rosofsky was lightweight, junior welterweight and welterweight champion, and a winner of the Silver Star in WWII. By what name was he known in the ring?

33. The first football coach at Harvard (1881) later owned the largest glove factory in the U.S. Name him.

34. What position did Johnny Kling play for the Chicago Cubs?

35. The Hart Trophy, named for Cecil M. Hart, is awarded to the M.V.P. in what sport?

36. Mendy Rudolph held what position in the N.B.A?

37. Which world championship did Maxie Rosenblum hold (1930-1934)?

38. By what nickname was Maxie Rosenblum known when he became an entertainer?

39. Benny Friedman was a member of the College Football Hall of Fame. For what team did he play?

40. Who was the U.S. baseball pioneer generally acknowledged to be the first paid professional in that sport?

41. Maurice Podoloff was the former commissioner of which sports association?

42. In what profession is Olympic gold medalist swimmer Mark Spitz trained?

43. Name the British Olympic gold medalist runner portrayed in the film *Chariots of Fire.*

44. Boxing champion Max Baer claimed Jewish paternity. What did he wear on his boxing trunks?

45. Hank Greenberg, twice M.V.P. in the A.L. and a member of the Baseball Hall of Fame, played first base for which teams?

46. Which All-Star Boston Braves baseball player, hit four grand-slam home runs in the 1950 season?

47. What three-time Olympic medalist in the featherweight division is also in the Weightlifting Hall of Fame?

48. Name the basketball player who was a member of the Hall of Fame and head coach of the Maccabiah basketball team (1977).

49. Who was the originator of the Maccabiah Games?

50. "Yussel the Muscle" managed Max Schmeling, the boxer. What was Yussel's real name?

THE BIBLE

1. The three Jewish forefathers are Abraham, Isaac and Jacob. Who were the four foremothers?

2. On which place did Moses receive the tablets?

3. Who are the legendary biblical, "best friends"?

4. How many books are contained in the Pentateuch?

5. How old was Jochebed when she gave birth to Moses?

6. Miriam of Magdela is popularly known as who?

7. Solomon was involved with 1000 women. How many were his concubines?

8. Name the son of King David who killed his half-brother to revenge the rape of Tamar.

9. What biblical story purports to explain the origin of different languages in the world?

10. Following the flood, which two birds did Noah send out to see if all was safe?

11. Name the two women in Abraham's life.

12. Who were the twin sons of Isaac and Rebecca?

13. How old was Moses when the pharaoh's daughter found him?

14. There is a zoo in Jerusalem which houses an unusual collection of animals. What does the collection represent?

15. Rachel died giving birth to Jacob's 12th son. Who was he?

16. Name the legendary queen who is said to have married Solomon.

17. From whom did King David steal Bathsheba?

18. Who was Bathsheba's noted son?

19. What is the shortest book of the Old Testament?

20. Who was the older brother, Moses or Aaron?

21. Who were Isaac's father and mother?

22. Who were Ishmael's mother and father?

23. Which son of David had long hair that proved to be his undoing, and why?

24. There has been an accepted practice among Jews not to give children names of Biblical persons who lived before Abraham. What are three exceptions to this?

25. Name the five Books of Moses.

26. For what biblical figure is the organization Hadassah named?

27. Name at least four of the Twelve Tribes of Israel.

28. Who was Abraham's chief adversary, considered one of the seven most notorious sinners of the world?

29. Terah was the father of which Jewish patriarch?

30. Pomegranates, wheat, barley, olives and honey — what do these foods have in common?

31. In the Book of Samuel, which four musical instruments are mentioned?

32. How old was Esther when she won the beauty contest?

33. In the story of Ruth, who was the mother-in-law and who was the daughter-in-law?

34. Joshua was the son of whom?

35. What were the occupations of Cain and Abel?

36. The Mezuzah and the Tefilin each contain a citation from which book of the Bible?

37. Who was Jacob's only daughter?

38. Which son of David raped his sister Tamar?

39. Who built the Tower of Babel?

40. How far was the Tower of Babel intended to reach?

41. Name the five Scrolls (Megilloth).

42. Who was the mother of Aaron, Moses and Miriam?

43. The dimensions of the Holy Ark are given in cubits. How did one measure a cubit?

44. How long, high and wide was the Holy Ark?

45. Which tribes of Israel originally settled the area now known as Jordan?

46. How long did Esther spend with beauticians before being presented to her future husband?

47. What famous Biblical Jew was said to be able to "turn water into wine"?

48. What kind of wood was used to build Noah's ark?

49. Name two sons of Joseph.

50. Who were Adam and Eve's three sons?

51. Which of Jacob's sons was red-headed?

52. The song claims that "Methuselah lived 900 years," but he actually lived 969 years. How long did Noah live?

53. Which son of Jacob did not have a tribe named after him?

54. Name two animals in the Bible that spoke. To whom did they speak?

55. Who were Noah's sons?

56. For which one of the following does the Old Testament supply a first name: Mrs. Lot, Mrs. Noah, Mrs. Moses, or Mrs. Joshua?

57. Rabbi Solomon Ben-Isaac is better known as who?

58. What was the chief contribution for which the above is remembered?

59. How long were the inhabitants of Noah's ark cooped up inside?

60. Who was Moses' father?

61. Which Biblical king is known for his

ability to write beautiful love poems?

62. In which book of the Bible do we learn of David's encounter with Goliath?

63. Who was the first king of Biblical Israel?

64. From which of the sons of Jacob did Moses descend?

65. What was the nationality of Delilah, Samson's beloved?

66. There is only one woman in the Torah who rose to a position of leadership among her people and led the Israelites in battle against an adversary. Who was she?

67. The fourth book of the Torah (Ba-Midbar) is called the *Book of Numbers* in English. Why?

68. Who is the Biblical character known to have had a coat of many colors?

69. In what book of the Bible would you find the phrase: "A good wife, who can find? She is worth more than rubies"?

70. What tree was planted next to the Tree of Knowledge in the Garden of Eden?

71. Name the king who reluctantly sentenced Daniel to the lion's den.

72. Which Jewish mother urged her son to deceive his father in order to receive his blessing?

73. How many rams horns were blown to topple the walls of Jericho?

74. Pishon, Gihon, Tigris and Euphrates are Biblical rivers that flowed where?

75. What did Adam and Eve do immediately after eating the apple?

76. What was the question that evoked the response: "Am I my brother's keeper"?

77. What was the profession of the woman who aided spies sent by Joshua to Jericho?

78. In the course of the exodus from Egypt, two bodies of water were parted. One was the Red Sea. Name the other.

79. How was Abraham related to Lot?

80. For what purpose did caravans of Ishmalites pay 20 shekels to sons of Jacob?

81. His Persian name was Xerxes and he won a victory in Thermopylae. What is his Biblical name?

82. Which king of Israel is considered to be the author of the *Book of Psalms*?

83. Name the King of Israel who is the author of *Ecclesiastes.*

84. How did the prophet Elijah ascend to heaven?

85. What was mined in King Solomon's mines?

86. What name was given to the son of the matriarch who laughed at the suggestion she would bear a child at age 90?

87. What rite was performed on all Israeli males after they crossed the Jordan River into Canaan?

88. On what Mountain did Moses die?

89. Which of the patriarchs of the Israelites has been described as the "son of a great father and father of a great son"?

90. Who was the first Jewish sailor?

91. Who was the Moabite woman who became the great grandmother of Israel's King David?

92. How long did Jonah remain in the body of the "great fish"?

93. Why did the pharaoh's daughter choose to name the baby she found in the Nile Moses?

94. What institution in Israel is named "Bezalel"?

95. Who was the Bezalel of the Bible?

96. The book of *Habakkuk* contains five curses; each begins with the words, "Woe to him." Who is being warned?

97. "...For where you go, I will go, and where you lodge I will lodge...." Who said this, and to whom was it said?

98. Which Prophet declared: "...and they shall beat their swords into ploughshares, and their spears into pruning hooks...."?

99. Where in NYC is the above prophecy carved into stone?

100. Can you complete the quotation begun in question 98?

101. Who was the first biblical father to worry about marrying off his unappealing daughter?

102. What father and son were circumcised on the same day and how old was each?

103. Name the biblical rogue who fathered both his own children and his own grandchildren?

104. Match these Biblical couples:
    1. Samson   (a) Sarai
    2. David   (b) Rebecca
    3. Ruth   (c) Jochebed
    4. Esther   (d) Asenath
    5. Amram   (e) Elisheba
    6. Isaac   (f) Delilah
    7. Abram   (g) Ahasuerus
    8. Lot   (h) Batsheba
    9. Aaron   (i) Pillar of Salt
    10. Joseph   (j) Boaz

31

STAGE AND SCREEN

1. Who played the role of Ari Ben-Canaan in the movie *Exodus*?

2. Because he was hungry, he sang in a Bowery restaurant in order to earn a meal. His song was "Rosie, You Are My Posie." Who was he?

3. *Waiting for Lefty, Awake and Sing, Golden Boy* and *Country Girl* are among his creations. Do you know his name?

4. Eric Weiss, a Hungarian born magician, was better known in the U.S.A. as who?

5. He created "The 2,000 Year Old Man," the TV series "Get Smart," directed and wrote *The Producers*. Who is he?

6. Which female singer brought down the house by ending her act with a rendition of "My Yiddishe Moma"?

7. Who played the role of Golda Meir on Broadway?

8. Name the movie based on the life of the distinguished U.S. Army colonel, who resigned his post to join the Israeli army.

9. An Israeli film won the American film critics award in 1964. Can you name it?

10. The actor who starred in *Salah* is known by his family name: Topol. What is his full name?

11. What Broadway play and radio program (circa 1940) dealt with a mixed marriage between a Jewish man and an Irish woman?

12. What was the name of the actress who played Molly Goldberg on radio and TV?

13. What other contributions did the actress above make to ''The Goldbergs''?

14. The singer who made his Broadway debut in *What Makes Sammy Run* is the son of a cantor. Who is he?

15. This actor has starred as the Jewish protagonist in both *Portnoy's Complaint* and *Goodbye Columbus*. Who is he?

16. Who wrote the novels on which the above movies were based?

17. In what Broadway show did Barbra Streisand get her professional start?

18. What actress converted to Judaism upon her marriage to a prominent U.S. playwright?

19. Name a former Israeli paratrooper who performs on TV and in nightclubs utilizing his psychic abilities, which he claims come from a distant planet?

20. A French Jew made his international debut as a mime in 1947 and created the character of "Bip." Who is he?

21. What is the name of the "Royal Family" of the Yiddish theater who found their way to prominence in the American theater?

22. Name four members of the "Royal Family" of the Yiddish theater referred to above.

23. What Jewish woman founded the Old Vic Theater Company in London?

24. What are the Folksbuehne, Artef and Vilna Troupe?

25. Who was the prominent Israeli woman portrayed by Ingrid Bergman in her last acting role?

26. Known as "The Look" in her early movie career, this Jewish actress was later named "Woman of the Year" by Harvard's Hasty Pudding Club. Who is she?

27. Name the three Jewish celebrities who, among others, were honored by

President Reagan in the Kennedy Center (1984) for life-long achievement in the arts.

28. Joel Grey inherited his famous father's talent for singing and dancing. Who was his performer father?

29. Which contemporary actor, director, screen writer and clarinetist was the moving force behind the films *Zelig, Annie Hall* and *Interiors*?

30. Who wrote the music and who wrote the lyrics to *Fiddler on the Roof*?

31. Which octagenarian began his career in show business with the "Pee Wee Quartet"?

32. In the play *The Dybbuk,* which character is inhabited by the Dybbuk?

33. A Jewish author-anthologist once introduced W.C. Fields by saying, "Any man who hates small children and dogs can't be all bad." Who is he?

34. Name the five daughters of Tevye in the Sholom Aleichem story *Tevye's Daughters.*

35. In the film *Animal Crackers,* who sang, "My name is Captain Spalding, the African Explorer/Did someone call me shnorer?"

36. Name the actor who played Jewish characters in the following movies: *The Fixer, The Pawnbroker* and *The Chosen.*

37. In early traditional Yiddish theater, *kuny-lemel* refers to the way any character other than the main character must be played. What manner is this?

38. His voice is that of Bugs Bunny, Porky Pig and Daffy Duck. Who is he?

39. Best known for his roles as Mary Richards' boss and an editor of a newspaper, he was also president of the Screen Actors Guild. Name him.

40. This Jewish actress was a leading lady of the Comedie Francais. Victor Hugo referred to her as "The Devine Sarah." Who was she?

41. In what movie did Joel Grey play master of ceremonies of the Kit-Kat-Klub?

42. After several years apart, this duo, known for "Mrs. Robinson," reunited to perform a concert in Central Park. Who are they?

43. She won an Academy Award for her portrayal of Billy Dawn. Who was she?

44. Son of a rabbi, this violin-playing comic is best known for being "frugal." Who is he?

45. What entertainer was nicknamed "Banjo Eyes"?

46. Name the five Marx brothers and give their stage names.

47. Which famous song and dance man, whose theme song is "Candy Man", converted to Judaism?

48. What is the name of Joan Rivers' mythical former best, best friend?

49. He began his career in the Yiddish theater and went on to star in Hollywood. One of his roles was Emile Zola. Who was he?

50. Who was the author of the play *The Dybbuk*?

51. Give the pen name of the author of *The Dybbuk.*

52. What year did *Fiddler On The Roof* open on Broadway?

53. Who sang the Tevye role in the first Israeli-Yiddish version of the production of *Fiddler*?

54. Who portrayed *Tevye the Dairyman* in the 1919 production of this play by Sholom Aleichem?

55. Name the professional Israeli dance troupe which presents dances of Yemenite Jews.

56. In the early Yiddish theater, an angel always wore white and capitalists smoked cigars. Which character always wore spectacles and which always carried an umbrella?

57. What is the name of Danny Kaye's

wife, a writer who created much of his material?

58. What man is credited with the founding of the Yiddish theater in America?

59. In 1948 the most popular TV program starred "Mr. TV." Who was this versatile Jewish comedian and what was the name of his show?

60. What actress starred in *Yentl* on Broadway?

61. What member of a prominent Jewish theatrical family played Tevye in the 1965 touring company of *Fiddler*?

62. Name the Jewish husband/Irish wife comedy team who have been active on radio selling Blue Nun wine and Encore frozen foods.

63. Who played Fagan in the 1963 Broadway production of *Oliver*?

64. In what Broadway musical did Molly Picon appear as Clara Weiss, tourist in Israel?

65. Who played opposite Gertrude Berg on Broadway in *A Majority of One*?

66. She won international fame for her role in the movie *The Shop On Main Street.* Who was she?

67. Barbra Streisand produced, directed and starred in a movie based on a short story by which Yiddish author?

68. Who starred in the original Broadway production of *Fiddler On The Roof*?

69. Mandy Patinkin played what role in the movie *Yentl*?

70. Which two actors played the role of "Uncle David" in the perpetual saga of *The Goldbergs*?

71. Who played Danny Saunders, the young man brought up in silence by his Hasidic father, in the movie *The Chosen*?

72. Who wrote the book upon which the movie *The Chosen* was based?

73. The movie *Funny Girl* and *Funny Lady* were based on the life of which Ziegfeld star?

74. Who was the second husband of the above star?

75. What was the radio name of the actress mentioned in the previous two questions?

76. This Jewish ballerina was born in London, became a Dame of the British Empire, director of the NYC Ballet and a Professor of Ballet. Who is she?

77. Who starred in the films *The Jolson Story* (1946) and *Jolson Sings Again* (1949)?

78. She supported Chaplain in *Limelight* and starred in *Charley, A Doll's House*

and *The Spy Who Came In From The Cold.* Who is she?

79. One of the hosts of the TV show *60 Minutes* was sued for libel by General Westmoreland. Who is he?

80. Adolph Zukor, founder of Paramount Pictures, established a different form of popular entertainment earlier in his career. What was it?

81. Which Jewish-Hungarian film producer-director was knighted for his contributions to British film (1942)?

82. Best-known for his roles in *Catch 22* and *The Russians Are Coming, The Russians Are Coming,* this actor began his career as a folk singer. Who is he?

83. Who was the star of the movie *The Adventures of Duddy Kravitz,* a story about a Jewish boy in Canada?

84. According to charitable custom, well to-do families boarded indigent male Talmudic students. Who is that student in *The Dybbuk*? In *Yentl*?

85. Who was Molly Goldberg's next door neighbor in the program "The Goldbergs"?

86. In 1936 a Yiddish film produced in Poland cast Molly Picon as a young fiddler masquerading as a boy. Name this successful Yiddish language film.

87. The son of a rabbi, he earned his nickname by graduating near the bottom of his class from Seward High in New York. He became a successful comedian and won a Tony for his performance in *Rhinoceros*. Who was he?

88. Moss Hart offered him a 38-second part in *Lady in the Dark* reciting the names of 54 Russian composers. Years later he won acclaim as a "Pied Piper" and ambassador of good will. Who is this talented actor-comedian?

89. He sings folk songs in Hebrew, Yiddish and other languages and he starred on B'way in *The Sound of Music*. Who is he?

90. What were the responsibilities of the *toomler* in Borscht Belt resorts?

91. Several of George Gershwin's songs were written under a pseudonym. What was it?

92. What is the name of the 1945 film that depicts the story of George Gershwin?

93. Who portrayed George Gershwin in the 1945 film biography?

94. Name the two actors who portrayed George and Ira as young men in the above film.

95. Which was the older Gershwin, George or Ira?

96. Which comic singer wrote "Hello Muddah, Hello Faddah"?

97. What revolutionary comedian in the 1960's used the famous "Jewish-Goyish" routine?

98. Name Elizabeth Taylor's Jewish husbands.

99. He was born Aaron Chwatt. He served as a singing bell-boy, which gave him his stage name. Who is this comedian?

100. The actor who starred in *Brian's Song* is known as "The Jewish Cowboy" because he is devoted to rodeo. Name him.

101. Leo Jacob's father worked on the *Jewish Daily Forward*. Leo played Barak Ben Canaan in the movie *Exodus* and Willie Loman in *Death of a Salesman*. What is this actor's stage name?

102. Name the National Theater of Israel.

103. The Jewish-Irish couple in the TV series "Bridget Loves Bernie" became a real life couple. Who are they?

104. Name the former Borscht Belt comic who is the host of an annual telethon on Labor Day.

105. Which Jewish actor starred with Barbra Streisand in the *Owl and the Pussycat* and with Ruth Gordon in *Where's Poppa*?

106. Who was the foremost interpreter of Gershwin, a celebrated cynic and host of TV's "Information Please"?

107. Name the former protege of Mel Brooks who played the frightened undertaker in *Bonnie and Clyde*?

108. The father gained prominence on "The Show of Shows," the son on "All in the Family." Who are they?

109. Name the Jewish actor who became the star of "Happy Days."

110. Who played Jess Rabinovitch opposite Lawrence Olivier in *The Jazz Singer*?

111. This actor, best remembered for his role as *Little Caesar,* was also a serious art collector and linguist. Name him.

112. Who was the actor behind the costume of the Cowardly Lion in *The Wizard of Oz*?

113. Which divine, outrageous Jewish performer won the 1976 Harvard Hasty Pudding Pot award for "Woman of the Year"?

114. Clifford Odets' play *The Flowering Peach* was the basis of a B'way musical which recounted the story of Noah. What was the name of the B'way show? Who was the male lead?

115. Who starred in *The Flowering Peach* by Clifford Odets (1954)?

116. Which pair of Jewish theatrical writers collaborated on *Wonderful Town*?

117. What was Ziegfeld's first name?

118. Name the Danish/Jewish comic-pianist best known for his renditions of a typewriter on the piano.

119. Best known for his one-man touring program of *The World of Sholom Aleichem* and a B'way production of *Fiddler,* this actor began his career on the Borscht circuit. Name him.

120. Which young Jewish musician noted for "romantic pop" aided Bette Midler on her road to fame?

121. At the conclusion of a lengthy preview of the Preminger film *Exodus,* which popular Jewish comic was said to have exclaimed, "Otto, let my people go!"?

122. Name the B'way musical in which Sid Caesar played seven leading parts.

123. This "great" of the Yiddish theater has been called a "Zoftig Jewish Hamlet" (1866-1939). Who was he?

124. **Be a *Shadchen* and make a match.**

    1. Daniel Barenboim
    2. Avrom Girsch Goldbogen
    3. Moss Hart
    4. Isidor Iskowitz
    5. David Daniel Kaminsky
    6. Jack Klugman
    7. Sidney Leibowitz
    8. Michael Igor Peschowsky
    9. William Samuel Rosenberg
    10. Gene Silberman (Silverstein)

    a. Fanny Borach
    b. Ida Cantor
    c. Jacqueline du Pre
    d. Sylvia Fine
    e. Edyie Gorme
    f. Catherine Holzm
    g. Elaine Berlin
    h. Gilda Radner
    i. Leonard Rosenbe
    j. Elizabeth Taylor

125. **And who were you before?**

    1. Henrietta Rosine Bernhard
    2. Nathan Birnbaum
    3. Issur Danilovich Demsky
    4. Samile Diane Friesen
    5. Ira Grossel
    6. Emanuel Goldenberg
    7. Leonard Hacker
    8. Irwin Kniberg
    9. Benjamin Kubelsky
    10. Isaiah Edwin Leopold
    11. Ivo Levi
    12. Joseph Levitch
    13. Laszlo Lowenstein
    14. Joan Molinsky
    15. Maria Peiser
    16. Lyora Rosenthal
    17. Shirley Schrift
    18. Bernie Schwartz
    19. Eric Weiss
    20. Asa Yoelson

    a. Jack Benny
    b. Sara Bernhardt
    c. George Burns
    d. Dyan Cannon
    e. Jeff Chandler
    f. Tony Curtis
    g. Kirk Douglas
    h. Lee Grant
    i. Buddy Hackett
    j. Harry Houdini
    k. Al Jolson
    l. Alan King
    m. Jerry Lewis
    n. Peter Lorre
    o. Yves Montand
    p. Lily Palmer
    q. Joan Rivers
    r. Edward G. Robin
    s. Shelly Winters
    t. Ed Wynn

SOUP TO NUTS

1. Name the golden, liquid food which is considered a "cure all" for whatever ails you.

2. What is the name of the Jewish organization established on many U.S. college campuses sponsored by the B'nai B'rith?

3. What is the Yiddish name for the long frock worn by members of the Hasidic sect?

4. What is the name given to the dais or platform in the synagogue from where the Torah is read?

5. What is the name of the International cosmetics empire founded by Charles Revson?

6. The shopping cart was invented by a Jewish multimillionaire who made his home in Oklahoma City, where he died in 1984. What is his name?

7. What is the name give to students of Jewish religious mysticism of the late medieval period?

8. What was the name of the Jewish secret intelligence organization that carried on pro-British spying operations during WWI in Syria and Palestine?

9. What Israeli military organization did Yigal Allon help found?

10. The Woman's Labor Zionist Organization of America offers social services to Israeli youth through vocational training. What is the name of this organization?

11. Where was the first Zionist Congress held?

12. Name the two cooperative bus companies in Israel.

13. Name the law which gives the right to every Jew to immigrate to Israel.

14. What chemical element in the periodic table is named after a Jewish scientist?

15. Peugot, Citroen, Renault — which of these French automobile companies is named for the Jewish industrialist who established it?

16. By what other name are knockwursts referred to in Jewish delicatessens in the New York City area?

17. What does the name *teller* have in common with a barber pole?

18. *Children of the Dream* is about the lives of children brought up in kibbutzim. Who is the author of this book?

19. What is the Yiddish expression corresponding to, "old wives tales"?

20. What is the phone number of the "Torah Hot Line" in NYC?

21. Who was the man credited with the modern revival of Hebrew speech and language?

22. Jews living in Arab lands adopted the Arab custom of using a *hamseh* as a talisman of good luck. What does *hamseh* mean and how is it represented?

23. How many years did it take to build the first temple?

24. What does a *hazzan* excel in?

25. Why should people who suffer indigestion from eating ice-cream love a man named David Mintz?

26. Name the Israeli underground organization which was led by Menachem Begin before the establishment of the state of Israel.

27. Name the genetic disease which affects only people of Ashkenazi Jewish ancestry.

28. What is the name of the folk cold-remedy that includes hot tea, honey, spices, schnapps, and more schnapps?

29. What ingredient present in bread must be left out of matzah in order for the matzah to be kosher for Passover?

30. What was the name of the Hungarian Jewish restaurant in NYC once listed among the top 50 restaurants in the U.S.A. by *Holiday* Magazine?

31. The names Kahn, Katz, Barkan, Kagan and Kaplan are derived from the same name. What is it?

32. Name the South African industry under Jewish ownership which served the millinery profession before WW1.

33. Name the kosher caterer hired by the White House to serve on the occasion of the 81st birthday of the Lubavitcher Rabbi, Rabbi Schneerson (1983).

34. Who was the technical director of the Los Alamos Project which involved the development of the A-bomb?

35. What is the name of the Hebrew language study system which provides new immigrants with intensive study?

36. What is the national emblem of Ethiopia?

37. What is the first Jewish fraternal society in America?

38. What is the Yiddish name for the fur hat worn by members of the Hasidic sect?

39. What are the Jews of Central and Eastern European origin known as?

40. Who developed the WISC, WAIS, WIPPSI test for measuring human intelligence?

41. What is the origin of the name *Ashkenazim*?

42. Who founded the Henry Street Settlement in NYC?

43. The well-known Jewish labor and fraternal organization is called the Workman's Circle. What is the Yiddish name?

44. What is the difference between a *Sherut* and other taxis in Israel?

45. By what name do we know the organization *Obshtchestvo Remeslenovo Truda,* founded in Russia 1880?

46. Every Friday night and on Yomim Tovim, services are broadcast from Temple Emanual, NYC. On what radio station can these be heard?

47. Jewish philanthropic organizations often distributed little boxes to Jewish homes for the purpose of collecting "change." By what generic name were these boxes known?

48. The eagle once served as a symbol of Jewish survival. It was used as a house sign and as a surname. What is this name?

49. What is Israel's domestic airline named?

50. What does *B'nai B'rith* mean?

51. Through what third country did Israel rescue the Ethiopian Jews?

52. The Israel Institute of Technology (Technion) was established (1912) with financial aid from two sources: one Russian and one American. Who were they?

53. Give the call letters of a Yiddish language radio station in NYC on which "Bintel Briefs" were read?

54. In January, 1950 an unusual natural phenomenon occurred in Israel. What was it?

55. What is the name given to a demon or transmigrating soul who inhabits a living being's body?

56. What agency is responsible for planting forests in Israel?

57. Who was the father of the atomic submarine, the admiral responsible for the Nautilus and one-time boss of President Jimmy Carter?

58. The world's largest and most celebrated hot dog stand which sold more

than 8 million a year in the 1940's and 1950's was located in Coney Island, NYC. What is its name?

59. To what famous NYC restaurant would you be headed if you were going to 138 Delancey Street between Suffolk and Norfolk Streets?

60. What is the main ingredient in *felafel*?

61. What is distinctive about the widely ramified family name Katzenellenbogen?

62. Many Spanish and Portugese Jews speak a mixed Hebrew and Spanish language. What is it?

63. For approximately how many people was Yiddish the vernacular at the beginning of the 20th century?

64. What dialect do the Ethiopian Jews speak?

65. What Israeli liquor is named after a cactus fruit?

66. What do these initials stand for: HIAS? JDL? JNF? UJA? IVO? ADL?

67. "*Tzu Gezunt*" in Yiddish, "*La Bri-oot*" in Hebrew — what sudden event elicits these responses?

68. The Hebrew name for Isaac is Yitzchak. What is the Yiddish version?

69. What was the name of Golda Meir's husband?

70. What is the native language of the Jews of Cochin?

71. What were the two syllables by which Molly Goldberg of "The Goldbergs" summoned her neighbors?

72. With the cooperation of what third country did the Israelis rescue hostages from an airport in Uganda?

73. What is the meaning of the Yiddish word *kishka,* a popular delicacy?

74. What is the stew made of carrots, prunes, and potatoes whose name also means "fuss and bother"?

75. What is the literal meaning of the name *Sephardim*?

76. What is the ingredient of a "two cents plain"?

77. In 1911 New York City's Public School #9 opened a kosher kitchen to feed 2000 pupils. How much did a kosher school lunch cost?

78. We were told in the 1960's we did not have to be Jewish to love a certain food product. What was it?

79. Which of the following ingredients would *not* be in the popular drink known in NYC as an egg cream: seltzer, chocolate syrup, egg, cream, milk?

80. The ship that carried Golda Meir to Israel in 1921 was named after an American Indian princess. Name the ship.

81. What was the name of the popular weekly English language radio program on Jewish topics (circa 1944)?

82. Name the largest "Kosher for Passover" discount supermarket in the world.

83. What fundamental change in admission policy occurred in the Jewish Theological Seminary in 1984?

84. The White House Office of Public Liaison sponsored an 81st birthday celebration in honor of the Lubavitcher Rabbi Schneerson. Which important guest was absent at this celebration?

85. The brothers Joe, Avi and Ralph Nakosh are Israelis who founded a successful clothing enterprise. Name it.

86. Name the oldest established kibbutz in Israel, referred to as "The Mother of Kibbutzim."

87. There is a group of Indian Jews who live mainly in Bombay and claim descent from Jewish survivors of a shipwreck that occurred 1800 years ago. What do they call themselves?

88. This schoolteacher's memoirs in-

clude his recollections of growing up in a large family rich in everything but money. Who is he?

89. Which *New York Times* cartoonist is *Nina's* father?

90. Who was considered the wealthiest Jew in the U.S.A. in 1792?

91. Name the Jewish biochemist who originated the word "vitamin"?

92. Who was Harry S. Truman's Jewish haberdashery partner in Kansas City, Missouri?

93. What is the profession of Menahem Meir, Golda's son?

94. Which Jewish family of Baghdad was called "The Rothschilds of the East?"

95. What was the name of the young boy (who later became the president of RCA) who picked up the last telegraph message from the *Titanic*?

96. The New York Stock Exchange grew out of the Stockbrokers Guild, founded in 1792 by 24 wealthy men. Who were the four Jewish men among them?

97. In whose honor did Queen Victoria declare Primrose Day a national holiday?

98. Columbia University School of Journalism was established due to the generosity of this man. He was also the publisher of the *St. Louis Post Dispatch*. Who was he?

99. What is the difference between a kibbutz and a moshav?

100. Who organized the Revisionists Zionist movement whose youth branch was known as Betar?

101. Which agency sponsors the periodical *Commentary*?

102. How old was Albert Einstein when he emerged from total obscurity to international fame with his Theory of Special Relativity?

103. Name the historic group that risked all to keep a few Jewish traditions and customs, yet went to church and pretended to be Christian.

104. Name the European family of bankers and philanthropists who, for over two centuries, formed the greatest financial dynasty in the world.

105. How old was Mordecai Kaplan, founder of The Jewish Reconstructionist Movement, when he died?

106. His family name may be found imprinted on many toilet paper and paper towel dispensers in public rest rooms. Who is he?

107. What is the common thread in the names: Ibn Abraham, Ben Abraham and Abramovich?

108. What was the name of the ship that carried the first group of Jews to New Amsterdam?

109. What is the name of the Hasidic sect that developed a rivalry with the Lubavitchers?

110. Introduced by Jacob Pollak, this discipline was widely used in Poland by Talmudic scholars when debating. What is it called?

111. By what acronym is the Baal Shem Tov known?

112. Who is the father of cybernetics and the author of *Ex-Prodigy*?

113. What is the name of the medical school of Yeshiva University?

114. A common "cure" in the Shtetl involved the placing of steam-heated glass cups on a patient's back in order to "suck away" the sickness. What is the name given to these cups?

115. If this is *Pesach* 1985, what year is it in the Jewish calendar?

116. In what two ways was Albert Einstein related to Elsa Lowenthal?

117. What are the two most ancient and common Jewish family names which are still in use today?

118. Who is the Austrian immigrant, founder of "The Literary Emporium" that developed into the largest chain of book stores in the world?

119. Which is the foremost educational in-

stitution of Orthodox Jewery in America?

120. What was the name of Pauline Koch's brilliant world-renowned son?

121. The national airline of Israel is named El Al. What is the meaning of the phrase "El Al"?

122. Identify the following delicacies made from chicken: (a) *helz'l,* (b) *gribenes,* (c) *poopik.*

123. What is the name by which the current Rabbinic Court of Law, with jurisdiction in civil, criminal and religious matters, is known?

124. To what Jewish college fraternity did Dr. Jonas Salk belong?

125. Where was the formerly all Jewish college fraternity Zeta Beta Tau founded (1898)?

126. What is the main difference between a bagel and a bialy?

127. The Israeli organization Magen David Adom is equivalent to what international organization?

128. One of the owners of the Marks and Spencer retail stores in England founded a research institute which later became the Weizmann Institute. Who was he?

129. *I Married Wyatt Earp* was written by "Sadie," the wife of the notorious gunfighter of the OK Corral. She was the

daughter of Sophie and Henry Marcus of San Francisco. What is her name?

130. This man invented the microphone and an early gramophone, and held patents for improvement of the telephone. Who was he?

131. "Barnato the Magician" was Cecil Rhodes' partner in the De Beers Consolidated Diamond Mines in South Africa. What was his real name?

132. How many letters are there in the Hebrew alphabet?

133. By what names are each of these delicacies known?
    (a) A Passover dessert made of matzoh meal and eggs, and fried in oil
    (b) A Near-Eastern confection made of sugar and sesame seeds
    (c) A flour, nut, honey and ginger sweet
    (d) A pudding made of noodles, eggs and oil

134. Name the psychiatrist who was at one time a disciple of Sigmund Freud and who counted among his works *The Neurotic Constitution.*

135. Name the two brothers, members of a prominent New York Jewish family, who became heads of the R.H. Macy store in 1896.

136. The oldest YMHA in existence is in NYC. When was it founded?

137. Where did the Levitt family build the first Levittown?

138. David and Igor, father and son, are world-renowned Russian-Jewish violinists. What is their family name?

139. In addition to apples and wine, what else goes into the *charoset* used in the Passover Seder?

TRADITION ... TRADITION

1. What does the word *chai* mean?

2. What is the numerical value of the letters *chai*?

3. What does the word *brith* mean?

4. How old should a baby boy be at his *brith*?

5. What is the official title of the person who performs circumcision?

6. May the ceremony of *brith* take place on Shabbat or Yom Kippur?

7. Legend tells of an unseen guest at the *brith* ceremony. Who is this?

8. Who is considered a *sabra*?

9. What has been the traditional manner in which Israel's Independence Day is celebrated?

10. How many sets of dishes does an observant family require for use on a daily basis?

11. It is necessary to redeem the first-born son of a Jewish mother provided she is not the daughter of a Cohen or Levy. What is the redemption ceremony called?

12. How old must the first-born son be at the redemption ceremony?

13. There are exceptions to the tradition of *Pidyon ha-ben.* Name one.

14. With what must the redemption be made?

15. What does the term used at all occasions of family festivities, *Mazel Tov,* literally mean?

16. What is the mitzvah of giving charity called?

17. What are the two disparate customs between the *Ashkenazim* and the *Sephardim* in naming newborn children?

18. The modern Jewish house of worship was originally called a temple. Today we interchange a Greek word which translates, "the place we bring together." What is the word?

19. A future groom is called to the Torah before his wedding day in a "calling up" ceremony. What is the Yiddish name for this ceremony?

20. It is traditional for the bride to wear a veil during the wedding ceremony. Of what is this custom symbolic?

21. What is the Hebrew name for the wedding canopy?

22. What is the name of the Jewish marriage contract?

23. What is the English translation of Yom Ha'azma'ut?

24. What does the word *mezuzah* mean?

25. What is customarily smashed at the wedding? (Careful here!)

26. In what language is the *ketubah* written?

27. What is a *shofar* made of?

28. On which two holidays is the *shofar* sounded?

29. What are the four names of the *shofar* blasts?

30. What is a Jewish divorce called?

31. In which room in a Jewish home is a *mezuzah* not necessary?

32. What does the Yiddish word *daven* mean?

33. What is the name of the morning prayer?

34. What term is used when deciding to immigrate to Israel?

35. What is the term used when one is called to read from the Torah at Temple?

36. What does the word *aliyah* mean?

37. What is the name of the person who does the calligraphy of the Torah?

38. According to Jewish tradition, the wedding ring has to fulfill three requirements. What are they?

39. What characteristic does a pig lack to be kosher?

40. When is *Birchat Hamazon* recited?

41. According to the Talmud, how much can be eaten without having to recite the *Birchat Hamazon*?

42. According to the laws of Kashrut, which one of the following pairs may not be eaten together?
    A. fish and meat
    B. eggs and chicken
    C. cheese and hamburger
    D. margarine and steak

43. What is the name given to the category of foods which are neither *milchik* or *fleishik*?

44. With the exception of Yom Kippur which is the most important holiday of the Jewish calendar?

45. What is the name of the afternoon prayer?

46. What is *schockeling*?

47. Traditionally women light the Shabbat candles; under what circumstances would a man perform this ceremony?

48. What is special about the Indonesian animal babirusa?

49. What does the ritual of *Havdalah* signify?

50. What is the name of the fringed garment worn during services?

51. What is a *tallit katan*?

52. What is a *kitel*?

53. The closest anyone has come to compiling a single legal code of law for the Orthodox Jew is a 16th century work by Joseph Caro. Name it.

54. An Orthodox Jew usually will adhere to the custom of allowing the beard to grow. He will not use a razor. What implement is permitted?

55. What is the name of the book used at the Seder table which tells the story of Passover?

56. Name the *minor* Jewish holiday which often coincides with one of the most important holidays for Christians.

57. "The Feast of Lots" is another name for what holiday?

58. What is done with *chametz* in preparation for Passover?

59. The days intervening between Passover and Shavuot are counting days; how many days are counted?

60. How many days between Erev Rosh Hashanna and Erev Yom Kippur?

61. Which of the songs sung at the Seder begins by telling about the purchase of a goat or a kid?

62. What is the name of the holiday where no leaven of any kind is to be eaten?

63. In which order are Hanukah candles set in the menorah, right to left, or left to right?

64. From which direction are the Hanukah candles lit?

65. There is a fast traditionally observed on the day before Passover; what is the name of the fast?

66. What did God drop from heaven as food for the Israelites in the desert?

67. What is the name of the citrus fruit, used on Sukkot, that looks like a lemon?

68. What is the tip of the aforementioned fruit called?

69. What is the name of the Jewish equivalent of Arbor Day?

70. According to the story of Hanukah, how many days did the one-day supply of sacramental oil actually last?

71. At the end of which holiday is it traditional to begin building a sukkah?

72. It is customary on Purim to exchange gifts of fruit and sweets with friends. What is the name of this gift giving custom?

73. During which period of the Jewish calendar are there restrictions against marriage, haircuts, concerts and dances?

74. What is the name of the food most commonly associated with Passover?

75. Why is *shemurah matzoh* different from all other matzoh?

76. In the Purim service, what prompts the congregants to make noise and shake their groggers?

77. Name the Hebrew month during which three major Jewish holidays are celebrated.

78. Name the three "Pilgrim Holidays."

79. What is the traditional ceremonial conclusion of the Shabbat meal?

80. What is a *mitzvah*?

81. What are the three traditional types of fish used in gefilte fish?

82. Name the two objects that are held in hand while saying a blessing in the Sukkah.

83. On what holiday is it customary to eat an apple dipped in honey?

84. What does dipping an apple into honey symbolize?

85. Identify the holiday that ends and begins the reading of the Torah in a single ceremony?

86. The lulav is held with two other kinds of branches. What are they?

87. What does Rosh Chodesh celebrate?

88. What is a *tzitzit*?

89. What holiday separates Sukkot from Simchat Torah?

90. In what special way are the names of Haman's sons recited in the reading of the *Book of Esther*?

91. Who is obliged to ask the four questions at the Seder?

92. What is a Mogen David?

93. What word do the *tefilin* straps form when properly wrapped around the hand?

94. What is significant about the number 613 in Jewish law?

95. In the draydl game played on Hanukah, what rules apply when the draydl lands on: (a) Gimmel (b) Shin (c) Hay (d) Nunn?

96. On which holiday are potato pancakes (latkes) traditionally served?

97. What is the name of the Hanukah candle that is used to light the others?

98. What is the difference between a *hanukiah* and a *menorah*?

99. According to Jewish law, what two fibers cannot be woven into cloth together?

100. What does the *charoset* symbolize at the Seder?

101. What does the "Minor Day of Atonement" (Yom Kippur Katan) celebrate?

102. What is the holiday for which both the home and synagogue are decorated with greens, branches and flowers?

103. At the entrance to a home, does the top of the *mezuzah* tilt inward or outward?

104. How many days into the Omer is the holiday Lag b'Omer?

71

105. At the Seder a glass of wine is poured for an expected special guest. Who is he?

106. On which day of the week is *tefilin* not worn?

107. What are the three *mitzvot* one must complete in the Sukkah?

108. What does the word *Seder* mean?

109. How many people are required to form a *minyan*?

110. Name the three items required to perform the Havdalah service.

111. At which meal is it permissible to encourage children to "steal" and what is it that is stolen?

112. What holiday is traditionally celebrated much the same as the non-Jewish holiday of Halloween?

113. What is the name of the partition that separates men and women in an orthodox shul?

114. Give the more common name for the bread of affliction.

115. During the Exodus a double portion of manna fell from heaven on Shabbat. How is this event commemorated every week?

116. How many plagues are cited at the Seder?

117. What ceremony accompanies the recitation of the plagues?

118. Name five of the Passover plagues.

119. What prayer is considered the most important in affirming Jewish faith?

120. In what language is *Kol Nidrei* recited?

121. What are the only two occasions when a Jew bows low at a prayer service?

122. What is it that is symbolically shed into water in the *Tashlich* ceremony?

123. Which is the "happiest" of the holidays in the Jewish calendar?

124. What event signals the end of Shabbat?

125. What are the items traditionally found on a Seder plate?

126. Traditionally when are the following foods eaten? A. *latkas* B. *kreplach* C. *hammantashen*

127. By what other name are the following known? A. Feast of Tabernacles B. Feast of Weeks C. Festival of Lights D. Fast of Esther

128. Commemoration of the various disasters which have befallen the Jewish people, specifically, the destruction of the Temple, occurs on the Ninth of Av. What is the name of this day?

129. The theme of Shabbat as a "bride" is enhanced by the singing of a 16th century prayer. What is the name of this beautiful prayer?

130. On which Jewish holiday is the traditional gift of *gelt* given to children?

131. What are the three meanings of the word *Shalom?*

CREATIVE ARTS

1. Who wrote the novel *Exodus*?

2. In which modern novel does the main character encounter conflict between his Jewish heritage and his artistic talent?

3. What is the name of the book by Maurice Samuels that tells the story which Bernard Malamud relates in *The Fixer*?

4. Name the editor of the journal *Commentary*.

5. Yehudi Menuhin and his sister often give concerts together. What is her instrument and name?

6. Where was Leonard Bernstein, composer of *The Jeremiah Symphony*, *Kaddish*, *West Side Story* and *Candide*, born?

7. Who was the famous cellist that at one time taught Golda's son Menachem to play cello?

8. Who wrote the once-popular Yiddish song "Bai Mir Bist Du Schein"?

9. Which poet wrote a moving narrative in memory of his dead mother, entitled *Kaddish*?

10. The Lincoln penny, the first coin bearing the head of a president, was designed by a Jewish artist. Name him.

11. Where would one find the masterpiece *Creation of Adam* by Michelangelo?

12. Who was the painter of *The Jewish Bride* and *The Rabbi of Amsterdam*?

13. For what novel did Barbara Tuchman win a Pulitzer?

14. Name four Yiddish language daily newspapers which flourished during the first half of the century.

15. Which of the above is the only one to have survived and is now published as a weekly?

16. Who was the Yiddish writer who gave the world the character, of *Bonche Shweig*?

17. What identical title did both I.J. Singer and John Steinbeck give to a literary work?

18. Which catalog of pertinent Jewish information have Richard Siegal, and Sharon and Michael Strassfeld edited?

19. Who was the Yiddish poet and author born in Lithuania whose outstanding work is his Yiddish version of the Bible?

20. What world renowned Vienna-born Zionist wrote the following: *I and Thou, Moses* and *Between Man and Man*?

21. Mayor Edward Koch of New York City wrote a best seller. What was the title?

22. Name the American born author, critic and patron of the arts who established a salon in Paris, where authors, artists and near-greats flocked.

23. Who is the novelist responsible for introducing us to *Augie March*?

24. Who created the immortal, "H*Y*M*A*N K*A*P*L*A*N"?

25. Translated as *Tuesday and Friday Courant,* the first Yiddish newspaper in the world was published in which city?

26. On Feb. 14, 1896, a book which was to revolutionize Jewish life and political thinking appeared in Vienna. It was written by Theodor Herzl. Name the book.

27. One of Picasso's earliest and best known works was a portrait of an American-born Jewish author known for the line, "A rose is a rose is a rose is a rose." Who was she?

28. Jan Peerce made his opera debut in 1938 as the Duke in *Rigoletto*. What was his stage name years before, used when he began his professional career?

29. When strumming his guitar and singing, this Israeli rabbi is known as "Israel's Pied Piper". Who is he?

30. In what historic novel does Bernard Malamud tell the story of Menachem M. Beilis?

31. This Hebrew-Yiddish author laid the foundations of an artistic Hebrew style and influenced Yiddish prose. His name is Sholom Jacob Abramowitch. What is his pen name?

32. (a) What is the name of the anthem that, when translated, begins, "As long as in a Jewish breast the son's stirring has not ceased..."?
    (b) What is the meaning of the name of this song?

33. What Hebrew poet wrote the words to what became the Israeli National Anthem?

34. Who was the editor-in-chief of the most popular Yiddish daily, *The Forward,* during the first half of the century?

35. "Yente Telebende" was a famous character in a Yiddish newspaper serial published in NYC invented by a humorous writer. His pen name was B. Kovner. What was his real name?

36. Who was the Yiddish dramatist, novelist and editor who founded the Farband Labor Zionist organization?

37. Saul Raskin (1878-1966) provided illustrations for 12 significant Jewish volumes. His 12th and last publication, *The New Faces of Israel,* was done with a then newly-developed implement. What was it?

38. Name the revived Jewish musical form which now consists of a blend of vocal, instrumental jazz and ragtime.

39. *Up The Down Staircase* was written by the granddaughter of Sholom Aleichem. Name her?

40. Which school of music was directed by the violinist Efrem Zimbalist?

41. How does the son of Efrem Zimbalist Sr. earn his livelihood?

42. In 1937, the songwriter Sammy Cahn translated the popular Yiddish song, "Bai Mir Bist Du Schein," for which group of female singers?

43. What is the name of the English language newspaper published daily in Israel?

44. Give the title of the novel written by Henry Roth, that portrays early immigrant life in NYC.

45. The wife of an Israeli diplomat wrote several scholarly reference books on Jewish topics, among which are *The Diaspora Story* and *Who's Who in the Bible.* What is her name?

46. What interpretation did David Pinski place on the term "Wandering Jew" in his novel of the same name?

47. What is the medieval interpretation of the term "Wandering Jew"?

48. Name the English language novel written by the editor-in-chief of the socialist labor Yiddish paper that not only belongs to the genre of immigrant fiction but explores the world of business.

49. Name the author of the above book.

50. Name the three Soyer brothers of the art world. Which two are the twins?

51. Name the American Jewish sculptress whose works include a bust of Louis D. Brandeis, a bas relief of Oliver Wendell Holmes and the popular *Boy and Bird* in the Boston Garden?

52. Who created the stained glass windows in the UN Secretariat and the murals in the Metropolitan Opera house at Lincoln Center, NYC?

53. Philip Roth wrote a collection of short fiction which won the National Book Award in 1960. Name the movie based on these stories. Who was the male lead?

54. The author who wrote *Al Aha-Vat Tzion (For the Love of Zion)* is considered to be the first Hebrew novelist. Name him.

55. Name the novel written by George Eliot in 1876 which advocates a homeland for Jews in Palestine.

56. What was the title of the autobiography of the first president of Israel?

57. Until his death in 1984, the tenor Jan Peerce was registered in the Musicians Union Local #802 as a player of what musical instrument?

58. The novelist who wrote *Mary* wrote in both Yiddish and English. What is his name?

59. "Der Alef-Beys" was the original title to what once-popular Yiddish song written by Mark Warshawsky?

60. The melody of the song cited in the previous question was later used in the film *Rhapsody In Blue,* which was based on the life of a popular composer. Name him.

61. Moshe Nader wrote a Yiddish version of the English poem *Old King Cole.* What was its name?

62. Which U.S. scholar, philosopher and professor of ethics wrote *Man Is Not Alone?*

63. The *Jewish Daily Forward* featured a widely popular "Letters to the Editor" column. By what name is the collection of these letters now known? Who was the editor these letters were addressed to?

64. Marc Chagall's stained glass windows were installed in February 1962 at the Hadassah Hospital in Jerusalem. What are the subjects of the windows?

65. Identify the French Sephardic Jewish family of artists that include Camille, George and Lucien.

66. What is the name of the New York-born sculptor who includes among his works the tomb of Oscar Wilde in Paris?

67. Which Italian-born Jewish painter is known for his portraits of long-necked women?

68. Which Russian-American violin virtuoso traveled to China and was filmed in the documentary *From Mao to Mozart*?

69. Who was the composer of *God Bless America*?

70. Which Jewish woman won a Pulitzer Prize for Literature in 1925? Name the book which won her the award.

71. I.J. Singer is the brother of I.B. Singer. Both are noted Yiddish novelists. Who was the older brother?

72. Which Jewish humorist founded Random House Publishing Company?

73. Jacob, Simca, David and Moshe shared the same profession. David and Moshe lived in NYC, Jacob and Simca lived abroad. What profession did these brothers practice?

74. What popular Christmas song was written by a popular Jewish songwriter?

75. Which Russian-born U.S. artist noted for his outstanding graphic work illustrated a popular Passover *haggadah*?

76. The man considered to be the greatest modern Hebrew poet is quoted as saying, "Translating from one language to another is like kissing one's sweetheart through a veil." Who is he?

77. Which two-hour montage documentary, broadcast via radio in 1979, was awarded several National Broadcasting honors as a captivating demonstration of the spirit of Judaism?

78. Which cantor was known as the "Jewish Caruso"?

79. Name the youngest musician to be appointed conductor of the New York Philharmonic.

80. *Appalachian Spring* won the Pulitzer Prize for which composer?

81. Which song written by Naomi Shemer won her the 1967 Jerusalem Prize? (It became the anthem of the Six Day War.)

82. What do Geula Gill and Shoshana Damari have in common beside the fact they are both Israeli?

83. Who was the Hungarian-American composer of over 70 operettas, of which *The Student Prince* and *The Desert Song* are the most widely known?

84. What profession do we associate with Moishe Oysher?

85. He created a Hebrew style of folk music, composed the opera *Jezabel,* the Symphony *Israel* and the cello rhapsody *Shlomoh.* Who was he?

86. A Jewish feminist quarterly which began publication in 1976 was named *Lilith.* What is the legendary role of Lilith?

87. How were the composer Felix and the philosopher Moses Mendelssohn related?

88. To whom did Leonard Bernstein dedicate his *Third Symphony*?

89. He earned his Ph.D in philosophy, served as an editor at the Jewish Publication Society, is an Orthodox rabbi and turned to writing fiction in the 1960's. Several of his popular novels became bestsellers. Who is he?

90. Name the traditional instruments of the Klezmer.

91. What musical instrument reigns supreme as the single most important instrument in Yiddish life?

92. This Czech Jew obtained a doctorate in law, worked in an insurance company and made contributions to literature in his spare time. His major works include *Metamorphosis* and *America.* Who is he?

93. Saul Bellow's "most Jewish book" allows the reader access to an American professor's private thoughts through his letters. The name of the professor is the name of the book. What is it?

94. Who was Arturo Toscanini's talented Jewish son-in-law?

95. Match the musician with his instrument.
    1. Benny Goodman   a. flute
    2. Stan Getz   b. harmonica
    3. Ziggy Elman   c. saxophone
    4. Herbie Mann   d. clarinet
    5. Buddy Rich   e. drums
    6. Larry Adler   f. trumpet

96. The earliest reference to music is found in Genesis IV. What is the name of the world's first musician?

97. In the Tel Aviv Museum of Art, a pavillion is named for a special lady of the cosmetic world. Who was she?

98. Who was the photographer who published (1984) *A Vanished World,* the pictorial history of European Jews, 1934-1939?

99. What do the following have in common: Yossele Rosenblatt, Berele Chagy, Aaron Lebedeff and Richard Tucker?

100. Name the American contemporary woman author who wrote of the "discovery of self" and shocked the literary world with explicit sexual references.

101. What was the "seed" from which Yiddish Theater developed in the 19th century?

102. What two famous tenors with the Metropolitan Opera Company were former cantors, and how were they related to each other?

103. What museum in Washington D.C. is named after a man who amassed his fortune mining uranium in Canada?

104. Who is the showman, nightclub owner and avid art collector who donated a splendid group of sculptures to the Israeli Museum in Jerusalem?

105. Name the biochemist who has published over 250 books, many of which are science fiction, and is author of *The Gods Themselves*.

106. For which novel did Saul Bellow win a Pulitzer Prize?

107. Soprano opera star Beverly Sills has a nickname. What is it?

108. He co-authored *You Can't Take It With You* and *The Man Who Came To Dinner* with Moss Hart. Who was he?

109. This Associated Press photographer took the photo of American troops raising the flag at Iwo Jima in WW2. Who is he?

110. This musician is known as "The King of Swing." Who is he?

111. Once married to James Taylor, this singer's father founded the publishing company of Simon & Schuster. Who is she?

112. Name the composer best known for his operetta *Tales of Hoffman.*

113. Who included the following inscription on the fly leaf of his utopian novel: "If you will it, it is no dream"?

114. A historic novel by James Michener has been described by critics as a "monumental and imaginative study of the old and new nation of Israel." What is the name of the book?

115. Which play by Arthur Miller won a Pulitzer Prize in 1949 and has had a successful rerun on Broadway in 1984?

116. Who received critical acclaim in 1984 for his lead in the play mentioned above?

117. Who is the trumpeter that leads the Tijuana Brass?

118. Rebecca in Sir Walter Scott's *Ivanhoe* is modeled after what real-life Rebecca?

119. Which American novelist wrote *Catcher In The Rye* and *Franny and Zooey,* part of the nine story saga of the Glass family, a family of Jewish-Irish origin?

120. What is the best known of Israel's circle folk dances?

121. Why was the legendary Talmudic character Honi-Ha-Meaggel likened to Rip Van Winkle?

122. Name the author who wrote biographical novels about van Gogh and Michelangelo.

123. The score to *Butch Cassidy and the Sundance Kid* won this songwriter an Academy Award. Who is he?

124. Who is the songwriter who won Academy awards for the scores to *The Sting* and *The Way We Were*?

125. Name the husband and wife team who wrote the song "The Way We Were".

126. Which Russian-born U.S. violinist, considered by some to be the virtuoso of the century, made his debut at age 13 with the Berlin Philharmonic and in Carnegie Hall at the age of 16?

127. Who is the creator of "Li'l Abner"?

128. Name the author of *For Two Cents Plain.*

129. This political writer, China scholar and Pulitzer Prize winner is the author of a series of books called *The Making of the President.* Name him.

130. One of the foremost publishing houses for Yiddish and Hebrew books was founded in Cincinnati, 1854. It later

relocated in Chicago and then New York. (a) What is its name? (b) Who were the founders?

131. Who described herself as *An Unfinished Woman* in her autobiography and was the author of *Pentimento* and *Little Foxes*?

132. This illustrator of children's books won a Caldicott Medal in 1964 for *Where the Wild Things Are*. What is his name?

133. *The Caine Mutiny, Marjorie Morningstar* and *Winds of War* were written by this contemporary American writer. Who is he?

134. Name the first Jewish artist to be commissioned by the Vatican. (He created a stained glass panel for the audience hall.)

135. This Jewish architect and his partner Louis Sullivan designed the Chicago Stock Market building, Carnegie Hall and several synagogues. Who was he?

136. In *Ulysses,* what does James Joyce name his Jewish character from Dublin?

137. The son of the world famous Polish-born pianist Arthur Rubinstein is an actor who starred in *Pippin*. He has appeared on TV in *Crazy Like A Fox*. What is his name?

138. Joanna Greenberg first published *I Never Promised You a Rose Garden* under a pseudonym. What was it?

139. The immigrant father and seven sons of this family made their fortune from copper and other metals. They endowed an art museum in NYC which is named for them. What is the name of the museum?

140. Three prominent Russian-Jewish violinists who immigrated to the U.S. during the first half of the century studied in St. Petersburg with the same teacher, Leopold Auer. Two of these were Jascha Heifetz and Mischa Elman. Who was the third?

141. Match Game. Who were they before?

1.	Alfred Caplin	a.	Sholom Aleichem
2.	Ellen Cohen	b.	Victor Borge
3.	Esther P. Friedman	c.	Al Capp
4.	Pauline E. Friedman	d.	Marc Chagall
5.	Jacob Gershvin	e.	Bob Dylan
6.	Alvin Morris	f.	Cass Elliot
7.	Jacob Pincus Perelmuth	g.	George Gershwin
8.	Solomon Rabinovich	h.	Ann Landers
9.	Borge Rosenbaum	i.	Herbie Mann
10.	Moshe Segal	j.	Tony Martin
11.	Belle Silverman	k.	Jan Peerce
12.	Herbert Solomon	l.	Beverly Sills
13.	Robert Zimmerman	m.	Abigail Van Buren

MOSTLY GEOGRAPHY

1. What is the Jewish population in the U.S. according to the 1980 census: a) 3.6 million, b) 5.9 million, c) 8.8 million?

2. In what four countries do most of the world's Jews now live?

3. What is the name of the international airport in Lod (Lydda), Israel?

4. In which city and state is Brandeis University located?

5. This Jewish bridge engineer designed over 400 steel bridges, including the Mackinac in Michigan and the Triborough in NYC. Name him.

6. Where is the birthplace of Louis D. Brandeis, Supreme Court Justice and Zionist leader?

7. The old city of Jerusalem once again became part of a Jewish State following what modern historic event?

8. Who was the Dizengoff for whom Tel-Aviv's Dizengoff Square is named?

9. Which Jewish communities constitute the Diaspora?

10. In what structure in the Hadassah Medical Center are Chagall's famous windows located?

11. Which is the most photographed street representing the characteristic early Jewish settlement in New York City?

12. Where did Noah's ark come to rest?

13. The story of Ruth evolved in the city where King David was born. What is the name of that city?

14. Which town is further north, Bethlehem or Nazareth?

15. The town of Ein Bokek on the shores of the Dead Sea has a unique geographic distinction. What is it?

16. The city of Haifa was built on what mountain?

17. There is a rugged cliff in the wilderness of Judea where 960 besieged Zealots made their last stand against the Romans. What is its name?

18. The lowest geographical feature in the world is shared by Israel and Jordan. What is its name and how low is it?

19. What are the precious ancient documents housed in the wing of the Israel Museum called "Shrine of the Book"?

20. Which city was the center of Jewish population in China during the Middle Ages?

21. The Israelis assisted in the construction of an airport they later invaded. What is its name and where is it located?

22. Approximately how many countries in the world have less than fifty permanent Jewish residents? a) 12, b) 35, c) 72, d) 115.

23. Name Disraeli's manor house on 169 acres in which he lived until he died (1881).

24. Where is the geographic point of highest elevation in Israel?

25. Canaan was described as a "land of _____ and _____"?

26. To which kibbutz did David Ben-Gurion retire at the age of 86?

27. For what purpose was Ellis Island used before it became a disembarkation point for new immigrants?

28. Jews pray on one side of the Western Wall; Arabs have a mosque on the other. Which of these people pray on the side where Solomon's Temple once sat?

29. In what section of which city is the world headquarters of the Lubavitcher movement?

30. Name Israel's harbor city at the north end of the Red Sea which has played an important part in the 1947 partition plan of the UN.

31. Which is the coldest, wettest region of Israel: a) Eilat b) Galilee c) Mt. Carmel?

32. Give the name and location of the 222-room country home of Ferdinand Rothschild.

33. Where is the Jewish National Home for Asthmatic Children located?

34. The Jewish community of Cochin was located in what country?

35. In what city and state did Adam Gimbel open the first American department store?

36. Name the kibbutz which became the subject of a book by Golda.

37. Name any three of the gates at the walls of the Old City of Jerusalem.

38. Which of the gates to the Old City of Jerusalem is closed and why?

39. What is the orthodox section of Jerusalem whose name in Hebrew means "One Hundred Gates"?

40. Name the bodies of water connected by the Suez Canal.

41. On which mountain is the Hebrew University located?

42. The Reform Judaism movement began in which country?

43. Where is the southernmost Jewish congregation in the world?

44. Approximately how many Jews were in Palestine at the creation of the State of Israel?

45. Approximately how many Jews were in Israel in 1984?

46. What important historic objects were found in the Qumran Caves?

47. What was the former name of the Catskill Mountain resort now known as Grossingers?

48. Name the knish emporium in which the Jewish intelligentsia of the East Side of New York gathered during the early 1900's.

49. What is the name of the Jewish family that owned Monticello (Thomas Jefferson's estate) before it became a national monument?

50. Stern College is the women's division of which university?

51. What is the significance of the address 112 Mercer Street, Princeton, New Jersey?

52. The Holy rock atop Mt. Moriah has significance to Jews, Christians and Moslems. What is its earliest significance in Jewish history?

53. The Wailing Wall was once part of what structure?

54. What was the former name of the Weizmann Institute?

55. On June 7, 1981, Israeli planes destroyed an atomic reactor located near which city?

56. Where is the Garden of Gethsemane?

57. What city in Biblical Egypt was assigned to the family of Joseph, the son of Jacob?

58. Name the world traveller who in 1286 described the strong commercial and political influence wielded by the Jews of China.

59. The transfer of 46,000 members of the Jewish community of Yemen to Israel took place between 1949 and 1950. What name was given to this effort?

60. In which present day country is the site where Noah's ark came to rest?

61. What is, approximately, the population of Lubavitchers in the world?

62. Name the town in Israel where Baron Edmond de Rothschild established a wine industry to provide support for early Israeli pioneers.

63. Who built the first temple in Jerusalem?

64. What is the name of the historic and traditional burial site in Israel?

65. The Catskill Mountain resort area in New York is known by what other name?

66. One of the hotels in the resort area of the Catskills has its own U.S. post office designation and zip code. Which hotel is it?

67. Name the four countries that border on Israel.

68. Approximately how many trees have been planted in Israel during the 80 odd years that the Jewish National Fund has sponsored the program: a) two million, b) 60 million, c) 140 million?

69. Name three bodies of water that abut Israel.

70. Michelangelo's statue of King David is in which city?

71. How long is the Jordan River?

72. In decending order, which five cities have the largest Jewish population in the U.S.?

73. Name the river that flows through the city of Tel Aviv.

74. In 1981 what percentage of the Israeli population was Jewish?

75. Approximately how many people in

the world consider Hebrew their everyday language?

76. Where is the oldest European synagogue still standing?

77. In what southern city was the first U.S. Reform congregation established?

78. Where is the oldest (1656) Jewish cemetery in North America?

79. What is the present name of Serge Koussevitzsky's estate in the Berkshire Mountains of Massachusetts?

80. Where was the first kosher butcher shop in North America established?

81. Where was Golda Meir born?

82. In Islamic tradition Kaaba, built by Abraham and Ishmael, is the holiest shrine. Where is it located?

83. In which Midwestern city did Golda Meir's family settle when they arrived in the U.S.?

84. Name the body of *fresh* water which lies at the lowest elevation below sea level.

85. What is the modern name of the body of water known in the Bible as the "Reed Sea"?

86. What is the biblical name of Amman, now the capital of Jordan?

87. When was Tel-Aviv founded?

88. Name the first skyscraper in Tel Aviv. How high is it?

89. What major university was established in Tel Aviv in 1965?

90. What body of water lies on either side of the Sinai Desert?

91. What is the telephone number of the Jewish Community Center of Tokyo?

92. Where and when was the first Jewish community in Florida established?

93. Name the major town in the Gaza Strip.

94. What Arab country now exists in the region known as Transjordan?

95. Name the ancient city that borders on the modern city of Tel Aviv.

96. Name the first city in the U.S.A. to establish two congregations by 1802.

97. The Hasmonean revolt began in the home town of the Maccabees, the heroes we remember at Hanukah. Name the town.

98. What city is said to be the Jewish village of Joseph, father of Jesus, and the town of Jesus's childhood?

99. The Jewish Museum of NYC was formerly the mansion of the wealthy

Warburg family. On what street is this museum?

100. The Orthodox Bar-Ilan University, named for Rabbi Meir Bar-Ilan, is located in which city?

101. Rembrandt lived for 26 years in the Jewish quarter of which city?

102. In which country is the Dura-Europos dig, site of an ancient synagogue with the oldest known biblical wall paintings?

103. Where is Rachel's Tomb?

104. These "Wise Men" are the subjects of folktales of naivete and foolishness. What is the name of their town?

PICTURE THIS

1. Where is this menorah located?

2. This menorah was a gift to the people
   of Israel.
   a) Who gave it?
   b) To whom was it given?

101

1. Which is the correct way to wear this amulet? (A or B)

2. When worn correctly, what does it say?

1. What seaport is this a picture of?

2. What is the dome in the foreground?

3. What is the name of the street in the center of this picture?

1. On what occasion would *all* the candles pictured be lit?

2. Which set of candles would you light first?

1. What two names are commonly given to this structure?

2. What three ancient buildings existed on the other side of this structure?

3. What religious building now exists on the other side of this structure?

1. What does the word on this plate say?

2. What food is traditionally placed on this plate?

3. On what two holidays would the plate *never* be used?

1. What is the name of this historic structure?

2. Where is it located?

3. What is its historic significance?

1. What is the Yiddish name for these objects?

2. What is the Hebrew name for these objects?

3. During what holiday are they used?

1. This is a picture of the ruins of what ancient structure?

2. Who built this royal citadel?

3. What is the name of the Jewish sect that was martyred on this site?

4. Who was the leader of this sect? 109

1. What do these ten letters stand for?

2. What does the congregation traditionally do when the ark is opened?

1. Who is this a statue of?

2. Where is this statue located?

1. This is a picture of what city?

2. What is the wall in the center?

3. From what ancient cemetery was this picture taken?

1. Who is the man on the left?

2. Who is the man on the right?

3. Which one served in the Royal Fusiliers (1918)?

1. Where would one find these sand-stone formations?

2. After whom are the pillars named?

3. What are they adjacent to?

1. What is the name of the synagogue that this arc frames?

2. Where is it located?

3. In what century was it built?

4. By whom was it destroyed?

1. Who is this man?

2. To what literary form did he contribute?

3. His former home is now a museum. In what city is it located?

1. Where is this structure located?

2. In what century was it built?

3. By whom was it built?

1. What is the actual name of this tower, commonly called "The Tower of David"?

2. Who built it?

3. In what city is it located?

1. Name this city.

2. On what body of water is the city's beach front?

3. From right to left, name the five hotels seen on the beach front.

1.   What is the common name of this picture of Isaac and Rebecca?

2.   In what museum would one find this portrait?

3.   Who is the artist?

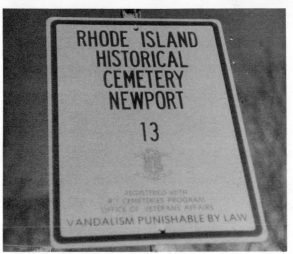

1. Which prominent poet wrote a poem about this historic cemetery?

2. Name the poem.

3. In what year was the cemetery consecrated?

4. Name three noteworthy men who are buried here.

5. One of the men buried here established the sperm oil industry in America. Name him.

121

AND MORE

1. Amy Eilberg of New York holds a non-traditional office within Conservative Judaism. What is it?

2. What is the full name of the German-Jewish bacteriologist who developed a blood test to detect syphilis?

3. Who was the winner of the 1908 Nobel Prize in Medicine for discovering a treatment for syphilis?

4. Name the professor, author and TV educator who is also an astronomer.

5. He was born to a Danish Jewish mother, developed the first modern model of the structure of the atom and won the Nobel Prize in Physics in 1922. Who is he?

6. Who was the wealthy financier, advisor to FDR and other presidents, often seen discussing high finance on a park bench with the great and near-great?

7. Who was the anthropologist-curator of the American Museum of Natural History who opposed the racial theory and supported cultural theories of anthropology?

8. Who is the man considered the "Father of Pediatrics," and the inventor of the laryngoscope in 1796?

9. Which U.S. biochemist and political activist shared the 1967 Nobel Prize for Medicine?

10. What words appeared on the first postage stamp issued by the State of Israel?

11. What was depicted on the first stamp issued by the State of Israel?

12. In 1946 Hermann J. Muller received the Nobel Prize for Medicine. What was his discovery?

13. We remember him for the oral polio vaccine he developed and as president of the Weizmann Institute of Israel (1969). Who is he?

14. Name the president of the Jewish Theological Seminary after whom many Jewish day schools are named?

15. In 1907 who won the Nobel Prize in Physics for measurement of the speed of light?

16. Name a prominent Jewish Harvard Law professor who defends controver-

sial causes and organizations. (One of his better known clients was Claus Von Bulow.)

17. His father was Jakob the Wool Merchant and his mother was Amalie Nathanson. His daughter is Anna, and the world knows him as the father of psychiatry. Who is he?

18. What is the name of the Hanukah song which utilizes the tune of "Rock of Ages"?

19. How does the Jewish calendar create a leap year?

20. What is the meaning of *Yom Tov*?

21. Contraptions designed to accomplish a simple task in the most difficult manner were the creations of which cartoonist?

22. Name the Russian-born anarchist portrayed by Maureen Stapleton in the film *Reds*.

23. To which Jewish congregation did George Washington write: "To bigotry no sanction, to persecution no assistance"?

24. Rabbi Theodore Lewis served the Touro Synagogue from 1949 to 1985. Where was he born?

25. What was the denomination of the U.S. postage stamp issued in 1982 in honor of the Touro Synagogue?

26. Which diminutive TV hostess signs off "Good night and good sex"?

27. What is the favored Russian soup made from a root vegetable and served with sour cream and boiled potatoes?

28. Which Hebrew month is added to the calendar on a leap year?

29. Irving Howe has written a study of the Eastern European immigrant to America in a widely popular book. Name the work.

30. Name the founder of Farrar Straus & Co., the publishing firm, and his grandfather, a Jewish U.S. diplomat of Teddy Roosevelts' day.

31. Name the U.S. family of entrepreneurs and social reformers whose name on a Boston basement store evokes frenzy in women shoppers.

32. By what name are the benevolent and social organizations which were formed by immigrants to the U.S. known?

33. What are the Hebrew words for "mother" and "father"?

34. What is the name of the song which is based on the 13 *Articles of Faith* formulated by Maimonides?

35. The French post office issued a stamp in honor of which great lady of the theater (1945)?

36. Bar Mitzvah—Bat Mitzvah. Which term applies to a Jewish female when she attains religious maturity?

37. What is the monetary unit in Israel?

38. The flag of Israel was created by David Wolffson. Upon what did he base his design?

39. Who wrote the poem *In the Jewish Synagogue at Newport*?

40. What is the appropriate response to "Shabbat Sholom"?

41. The brothers Levi, Samuel and Jacob Szemanski have an alley west of Broadway in NYC named for them. What is the name of the alley?

42. The vocabulary of the Old Testament contained 7,704 words. Approximately how many words have been coined since the modern revival of Hebrew: a) 10,000, b) 25,000, c) 50,000?

43. Name the airport museum that houses a significant collection of Judaica.

44. Name the Jewish physician who was editor of the AMA Journal for 25 years (1924-49).

45. The Israeli Army exempts three categories of people from service for

reasons other than health or national security. What are the three categories?

46. The Archeological and Biblical Wing of the Israel Museum was founded by the Bronfman family. Which Canadian company is owned by this family?

47. How many sons joined Meyer Guggenheim, the industrialist, in his mining business?

48. Identify each of the following sons of Meyer Guggenheim:
a) the ambassador to Cuba in 1929;
b) the founder of a free dental clinic in New York; and
c) the founder of a museum in New York?

49. Name the Canadian architect who invented the concept of *habitat.*

50. What is an appropriate response to "Shalom Aleichem"?

ANSWERS

HISTORY AND POLITICS

1. May 14, 1948

2. Asser Levy

3. Herbert Lehman

4. Samuel Gompers

5. 1948

6. Charles Orde Wingate

7. Herbert Samuel

8. Abraham Ribicoff

9. Walter H. Annenberg

10. Benjamin Disraeli

11. Maxim Litvinoff

12. Harry Ellis Dickson

13. Francis Salvador

14. Middlesex

15. Hayim Solomon

16. James Madison

17. Zalman Shazar

18. Theodore Roosevelt

19. *The Jewish Advocate*

20. David Dubinsky

21. King Farouk

22. Woodrow Wilson

23. *The Day (Der Tag)*

24. Gerard Swope

25. Herbert B. Swope, editor of *The World*

26. Felix Frankfurter

27. Moses Maimonides

28. Baruch Spinoza

29. Yitzhak Shamir

30. Leviticus XXV:10

31. Teddy Kollek

32. Louis D. Brandeis, Benjamin N. Cardozo, Felix Frankfurter, Arthur Goldberg and Abe Fortas

33. Lionel Walter Rothschild

34. Uriah P. Levy

35. It barred Jews from the Tennessee Department of the Army.

36. Francis Salvador

37. Lord Reading

38. Anwar Sadat

39. Adolpheus S. Solomon

40. Samuel Gompers

41. Six Day War—1967

42. David Marcus

43. Robert Briscoe

44. Harry S. Truman

45. An elaborate Torah scroll and case

46. Amos Lawrence and Judah Tuoro

47. Uganda

48. Argentina

49. Outside the city of Curacao, Dutch West Indies

50. Newport, Rhode Island

51. The Vilna Gaon (Elija Zalman)

52. Justice of the Supreme Court

53. Jacobo Timerman

54. Nebuchadnezzar

55. Bella Abzug

56. Mordecai M. Kaplan

57. del Vecchio

58. Napoleon

59. Gershom Mendes Seixas

60. 1492

61. Abba Eban

62. Isaac Artom

63. Herbert Lehman

64. Carl Bernstein

65. David Ben-Gurion, Moshe Sharett, Golda Meir, Itzhak Rabin, Menachem Begin, Yitzach Shamir and Shimon Peres

66. The Balfour Declaration

67. Moshe Sharett

68. Five

69. Judah Benjamin

70. Venice, Italy in 1522

71. Benjamin Natanyahu

72. Milton Shapp

73. 1939 White Paper

74. Abraham Lincoln

75. Stern College of Yeshiva University

76. Pierre Mendes-France

77. Ephraim Katzir

78. Morris B. Abram and Evelyn E. Handler

79. Itzhak Rabin

80. Yom Kippur — 1973

81. Abe Beame

82. Chaim Herzog

83. Michael Comay

84. Leon Trotsky (1879-1940)

85. 120

86. 133 C.E.

87. Menachem Begin and Anwar Sadat

88. Alfred Dreyfus

89. Ho Chi Minh offered a corner of Vietnam.

90. 2,000

91. Sir George Jessel (1873)

92. President of World Zionist Organization

93. Mt. Sinai, NYC (originally "Jews Hospital"), 1852

94. Hebrew Union College

95. Island of Curacao (1732)

96. David Emanual

97. David Yulee (D.-Florida, 1845-1861)

98. Asser Levy of New Amsterdam

99. Jacob Barsimon

100. Judah Monis

101. Louis D. Brandeis

102. Chaim Weizmann, Izhak Ben Zvi, Zalman Shazar, Ephraim Katzir, Yitzhak Navon and Chaim Herzog

103. Straits of Tiran

104. Menachem Begin, Anwar Sadat and Jimmy Carter

105. Hillel (the elder)

106. Brandeis University

107. Spain and Portugal

108. "Circuit Riding Rabbi Bus"

109. The enlightenment movement in Europe

110. Simon M. Levi of Maryland (1801)

111. The Baal Shem-Tov

112. Christopher Columbus

113. Jacob Frankel (Philadelphia 1862)

114. The rescue and relocation of the Ethiopian Jews

115. Henrietta Szold

116. Medical doctor (1656)

117. Henry Morgenthau Sr., U.S. Ambassador to Turkey

118. Mordecai Manuel Noah. The colony was to be *Ararat*.

119. Bess Meyerson (1945)

120. Albert Einstein

121. Sir Edmund Allenby

122. Adolph Sutro

123. Josephus Flavius

124. Masada

125. Yigal Allon

126. Abbie Hoffman and Jerry Rubin

127. Rabbi Isaac M. Wise

128. Riva Mor-Messinger

129. Sally Jane Prisand (1972)

130. Sir Moses Montefiore

131. She serves as cantor.

132. Esperanto

133. He was an oculist.

134. Ariel Sharon

135. 1. D   6. C
     2. F   7. E
     3. I   8. A
     4. G   9. H
     5. B

GOOD SPORTS

1. The game was played on Yom Kippur and he refused to participate.

2. Gregg Adleman

3. Amy Alcott

4. Boxing

5. Moe Berg (Dodgers, White Sox, Red Sox, Indians)

6. Intelligence agent

7. Chess

8. He was an umpire.

9. Samuel Weiss

10. The Cincinnati Reds

11. Nat Holman

12. Table tennis

13. Al Schacht

14. Wrestling

15. Baltimore Colts

16. Mike Epstein

17. Arnold Jacob "Red" Auerbach

18. Gladys Heldman

19. Barney Dreyfuss

20. Howard Cosell

21. Soccer

22. Boxing

23. Erskine Mayer

24. Sidney Luckman

25. Charles "Buddy" Myers

26. Emanuel Lasker

27. The Maccabiah

28. The Harlem Globetrotters

29. Dick Savitt and Herb Flam

30. Rod Carew

31. Handball

32. Barney Ross

33. Lucius N. Littauer

34. Catcher

35. Hockey

36. Referee

37. Light heavyweight

38. "Slapsie-Maxie"

39. University of Michigan

40. Lipman E. Pike, Philadelphia Athletics, 1866

41. N.B.A.

42. Dentistry

43. Harold M. Abrahams

44. The Star of David

45. Detroit Tigers (1933-1946) and Pittsburg Pirates

46. Sid Gordon

47. Isaac (Ike) Berger

48. Adolph Schayes

49. Yosef Yekutieli

50. Joe Jacobs

THE BIBLE

1. Sarah, Rebecca, Leah and Rachel

2. Mt. Sinai

3. Jonathan and David

4. Five

5. 130 years old

6. Mary Magdalene

7. 300

8. Absalom

9. The story of the Tower of Babel

10. The raven and the dove

11. Sarah and Hagar

12. Jacob and Esau

13. Three months old

14. Animals that are mentioned in the Bible. All are indigenous to Israel.

15. Benjamin

16. Queen of Sheba

17. Uriah

18. King Solomon

19. Obadiah

20. Aaron

21. Abraham and Sarah

22. Hagar and Abraham

23. Absalom was killed when his hair became entangled in a tree, enabling Joab to kill him.

24. Hava (Eve), Noah, and Hanoch (Enoch)

25. Genesis, Exodus, Leviticus, Numbers, and Deuteronomy

26. Queen Esther

27. Reuben, Simeon, (Levi), Judah, Issachar, Zebulun, Benjamin, Dan, Naphtali, Gad, Asher, Ephraim, and Manasseh

28. Nimrod (associated with Amraphel, Gen. 14:1)

29. Abraham

30. They were mentioned in the bible (Deut. 8:8).

31. Harps, drums, sistra and cymbals

32. 40

33. Naomi was the mother-in-law; Ruth was the daughter-in-law.

34. Nunn

35. Cain was a hunter and Abel a shepherd-farmer.

36. Deuteronomy

37. Dinah

38. Amnon

39. "Families of the sons of Noah."

40. Heaven

41. Song of Songs, Ruth, Lamentations, Ecclesiastes, and Esther

42. Jochebed

43. From the elbow to the tip of the middle finger

44. 2½ long by 1½ wide by 1½ high (in cubits)

45. Reuben, Gad and half the tribe of Menasseh

46. 12 months

47. Jesus

48. Gopher or cedar wood

49. Ephraim and Manasseh

50. Cain, Abel and Seth

51. Esau

52. 950 years

53. Joseph

54. The ass spoke to Balaam; the snake to Eve.

55. Shem, Ham and Japhet

56. Mrs. Moses (Zipporah)

57. Rashi

58. Biblical and Talmudic commentary

59. One year

60. Amram

61. David

62. Samuel

63. Saul

64. Levi

65. Philistine

66. Deborah

67. It begins with the story of the census taken by Moses when the Israelites left Egypt.

68. Joseph

69. Proverbs

70. The Tree of Life

71. Darius (the Mede)

72. Rebecca urged Jacob to deceive Isaac.

73. Seven

74. In the Garden of Eden

75. "Sew girdles of fig leaves."

76. "Where is Abel thy brother?"

77. She was a harlot.

78. The Jordan River

79. Lot was his nephew.

80. To buy Joseph

81. Ahasuerus

82. David

83. Solomon

84. In a chariot of fire

85. Copper

86. Isaac, which implies "laughter" in Hebrew

87. Circumcision

88. Mt. Nebo

89. Isaac

90. Noah

91. Ruth

92. Three days

93. Moshe (Moses) is derived from the Hebrew, "to draw." ("I drew him out of the water." Exodus II:10)

94. An academy of arts and crafts in Jerusalem

95. He was the head artisan who constructed the tabernacle.

96. Oppressors of animals or humans

97. Ruth to Naomi

98. Isaiah (2:4)

99. On a wall at the entrance to the United Nations building

100. "...and they shall beat their swords into ploughshares, and their spears into pruning hooks. Nations shall not lift up sword against nation, neither shall they learn war anymore."

101. Laban (Gen. 29:26)

102. Abraham at 99 and Ishmael at 13 (Gen. 17:26)

103. Lot (Gen. 19)

104.
1. f	6. b
2. h	7. a
3. j	8. i
4. g	9. e
5. c	10. d

STAGE AND SCREEN

1. Paul Newman

2. Al Jolson

3. Clifford Odets

4. Harry Houdini

5. Mel Brooks

6. Sophie Tucker

7. Ann Bancroft

8. *Cast A Giant Shadow*

9. *Salah Shabati*

10. Hayyim Topol

11. *Abie's Irish Rose*

12. Gertrude Berg

13. She wrote and directed the productions.

14. Steve Lawrence

15. Richard Benjamin

16. Philip Roth

17. *I Can Get It For You Wholesale*

18. Marilyn Monroe

19. Uri Geller

20. Marcel Marceau

21. The Adlers

22. Jacob, Stella, Luther and Celia

23. Lillian M. Baylis

24. Yiddish theater repertories

25. Golda Meir

26. Lauren Bacall

27. Arthur Miller, Isaac Stern and Danny Kaye

28. Mickey Katz

29. Woody Allen

30. Jerry Bock wrote the music and Sheldon Harnick wrote the lyrics.

31. George Burns

32. Leah, the bride

33. Leo Rosten

34. Tzeitel, Hodel, Chava, Schprintze and Beilke

35. Groucho Marx

36. Rod Steiger

37. Ignorant and clownish

38. Mel Blanc

39. Ed Asner

40. Sarah Bernhardt

41. *Cabaret*

42. Paul Simon and Art Garfunkle

43. Judy Holliday

44. Jack Benny

45. Eddie Cantor

46. Leonard - Chico
    Julius - Groucho
    Adolph - Harpo
    Milton - Gummo
    Herbert - Zeppo

47. Sammy Davis Jr.

48. Heidi Abromowitz

49. Paul Muni

50. Solomon Seinwil Rapoport

51. S. An-Sky (Ansky)

52. 1964

53. Shmuel Rudenski

54. Maurice Schwartz

55. Inbal

56. Doctors wore spectacles; marriage brokers carried umbrellas.

57. Sylvia Fine

58. Abraham Goldfaden

59. Milton Berle — "The Texaco Star Theater"

60. Tovah Feldshu

61. Luther Adler

62. Jerry Stiller and Ann Meara

63. Clive Revill

64. *Milk and Honey*

65. Sir Cedric Hardwicke

66. Ida Kaminska

67. Isaac Bashevis Singer

68. Zero Mostel

69. Avigdor

70. Menasha Skulnick and Eli Mintz

71. Robby Benson

72. Chaim Potok

73. Fanny Brice

74. Billy Rose

75. Baby Snooks

76. Alicia Markova

77. Larry Parks

78. Claire Bloom

79. Mike Wallace

80. The penny arcade

81. Alexander Korda

82. Alan Arkin

83. Richard Dreyfuss

84. Chonen in *The Dybbuk* and Avigdor in *Yentl*

85. Mrs. Bloom

86. *Yidl Mitn Fidl*

87. Zero Mostel

88. Danny Kaye

89. Theodor Bikel

90. "Mix it up" or keep the patrons happy by entertaining them

91. Arthur Francis

92. *Rhapsody In Blue*

93. Robert Alda

94. Mickey Roth and Darryl Hickman

95. Ira

96. Allen Sherman

97. Lenny Bruce

98. Mike Todd and Eddie Fisher

99. Red Buttons

100. James Caan

101. Lee J. Cobb

102. Habimah

103. David Birney and Meridith Baxter Birney

104. Jerry Lewis

105. George Segal

106. Oscar Levant

107. Gene Wilder

108. Carl and Rob Reiner

109. Henry Winkler ("The Fonz")

110. Neil Diamond

111. Edward G. Robinson

112. Bert Lahr (Bert Lahrheim)

113. Bette Midler

114. *Two By Two* starred Danny Kaye

115. Menasha Skulnick

116. Betty Comden and Adolf Green

117. Florenz (Flo)

118. Victor Borge

119. Herschel Bernardi

120. Barry Manilow

121. Mort Sahl

122. *Little Me*

123. Boris Thomashefsky

124.
1. c.	Daniel Barenboim - Jaqueline du Pre
2. j.	Mike Todd - Elizabeth Taylor
3. f.	Moss Hart -Kitty Carlisle
4. b.	Eddie Cantor - Ida Cantor
5. d.	Danny Kaye - Sylvia Fine
6. i.	Jack Klugman - Tony Randall
7. e.	Steve Lawrence - Eydie Gorme
8. g.	Mike Nichols - Elaine May
9. a.	Billy Rose - Fanny Brice
10. h.	Gene Wilder - Gilda Radner

125.
1. b	6. r	11. o	16. h
2. c	7. i	12. m	17. s
3. g	8. l	13. n	18. f
4. d	9. a	14. q	19. j
5. e	10. t	15. p	20. k

SOUP TO NUTS

1. Chicken soup

2. The Hillel Foundation

3. *Kapotah*

4. *Bimah*

5. Revlon

6. Sylvan N. Goldman

7. Cabbalists

8. Nili

9. Palmach

10. Pioneer Women

11. Basel, Switzerland (1897)

12. Egged and Dan

13. The Law of Return

14. Einsteinium (#99)

15. Citroen. Named for Andre Gustav Citroen

16. "Specials"

17. A *teller* was a plate that identified the barber-surgeon in eastern Europe.

18. Bruno Bettelheim

19. *Bubeh meisehs*

20. (212) 960-5450

21. Eliezer Ben Yehuda

22. It means five and it is represented by a palm and five fingers.

23. Seven (Midrash in I Kings Ch: 3)

24. Singing

25. He developed an ice-cream-like dessert called Tofutti, which is lactose and cholesterol free (and parve!).

26. Irgun Tsvai Leumi

27. Tay-Sachs

28. "Gogle mogle"

29. Yeast

30. Moskowitz and Lupowitz

31. Cohen

32. The ostrich-feather industry

33. Eddie Mermelstein of Crown Heights, Brooklyn, New York

34. Robert Oppenheimer

35. Ulpan System of the Jewish Agency

36. The Lion of Judah

37. B'nai B'rith

38. Shtreiml

39. Ashkenazim

40. David Wechsler

41. It first appears in Genesis 10:3 and was applied to Germans in the 9th century.

42. Lillian Wald

43. Arbeiter Ring

44. Sherut offers shared rides at a fixed price

45. O.R.T. (Society for the Encouragement of Handicrafts)

46. WQXR

47. *Pushkas* (or *pishkes* if you hailed from Galizia)

48. Adler

49. Arkia

50. Sons of the Covenant

51. Sudan

52. Jacob Schiff and the Wissotsky estate in Moscow

53. WEVD

54. Snowfall covered the country, including the coastal plain

55. A *dybbuk*

56. Jewish National Fund

57. Admiral Hyman Rickover

58. "Nathan's Famous"

59. Ratner's

60. Chick peas

61. It is the longest Jewish family name.

62. Ladino

63. 11 million

64. Amharic

65. Sabra

66. Hebrew Immigrants Aid Society
    Jewish Defense League
    Jewish National Fund
    United Jewish Appeal
    Yiddisher Visenshaftlikher Institute
    Anti-Defamation League (of B'nai B'rith)

67. A sneeze

68. Itzik

69. Morris Meyerson

70. Malayalam

71. "Yoo hoo!"

72. Kenya

73. Intestines

74. *Tsimmes*

75. People from Spharad ("Spain" in Hebrew)

76. Seltzer

77. Three cents

78. Levy's Bread

79. Egg and cream

80. *Pocahontas*

81. "The Eternal Light"

82. The Weitz Supermarket, East Meadow, Long Island

83. Women could now become rabbis.

84. Rabbi Schneerson — he never leaves his headquarters in Brooklyn

85. Jordache

86. Degania (1909)

87. Bene Israel

88. Sam Levenson

89. Al Hirschfeld

90. Ephraim Hart, partner to John Jacob Astor

91. Casimir Funk

92. Eddie Jacobson

93. Cellist—director of the Israel Conservatory of Music.

94. Sassoon family

95. David Sarnoff

96. Ephraim Hart, Isaac Gomez, Alexander Zuntz and Benjamin Seixas

97. Benjamin Disraeli

98. Joseph Pulitzer

99. A kibbutz operates as a collective while a moshav is a cooperative.

100. Vladimir Jabotinsky

101. American Jewish Committee

102. 26 years old

103. Marranos (Spain, Portugal, Mexico)

104. Rothschild

105. 102

106. James Zellerbach of the Crown Zellerbach Corp.

107. They denote "The son of Abraham."

108. *St. Charles*

109. The Satmars

110. *Pilpul*

111. Besht

112. Norbert Wiener

113. The Albert Einstein Medical School

114. *Bonkkes*

115. 5745

116. She was his wife and cousin.

117. Cohen and Levy

118. August Brentano

119. Yeshiva University in NYC

120. Albert Einstein

121. "On High"

122. (a) Stuffed neck, (b) cracklings, (c) gizzard

123. Bet(h) Din

124. Tau Epsilon Phi

125. City College of New York

126. The bagel has a hole; the bialy is chewier. (They both taste great with cream cheese.)

127. The Red Cross

128. Israel Sieff

129. Josephine Sarah Marcus Earp (1861-1944)

130. Emile Berliner

131. Barnett Isaacs

132. 22

133. (a) *Chremzlach* (b) *halvah* (c) *tayglach* (d) *lokshenkugel*

134. Alfred Adler

135. Nathan and Isidor Straus

136. 1874

137. Long Island, New York

138. Oistrakh

139. Nuts

TRADITION . . . TRADITION

1. Alive (life)

2. 18

3. Covenant

4. Traditionally, eight days old

5. Mohel

6. Yes

7. The Prophet Elijah

8. A native born-Israeli

9. Military parades

10. Two: one set for milk and one set for meat

11. *Pidyon ha ben*

12. At least 30 days

13. Sons of priests and Levites;
    babies born in Caesarian operations;
    or
    an adult who had not been redeemed

as an infant may redeem himself.

14. Coins worth five shekels

15. Good luck, (May your life be crowned with good fortune.)

16. *Tzedakah*

17. The *Sephardim* may name a child after someone still living; the *Ashkenazim* only name a baby in memory of a deceased.

18. Synagogue

19. *Aufruf*

20. Rebecca was veiled in her wedding ceremony to Isaac.

21. The *chupah*

22. A *ketubah*

23. Independence Day

24. Doorpost

25. A glass

26. Aramaic

27. A ram's horn

28. Rosh Hashanna and Yom Kippur

29. Tekiah, Shevarim, Teruah and Tekiah Gedolah

30. A *Get*

31. The bathroom

32. To pray

33. *Shacharit*

34. *Aliyah*

35. *Aliyah*

36. To go up.

37. A *sofer* (scribe)

38. It must be of a single piece of metal, belong to the groom and have monetary value.

39. The pig doesn't chew its cud.

40. After meals

41. Any quantity "smaller than an olive."

42. C

43. Parve

44. Shabbat

45. *Mincha*

46. The rocking back and forth while praying

47. In the absence of a woman

48. It is similar in look and taste to a pig, but it chews its cud and therefore,

may be kosher!

49. The separation of a holy day from an ordinary day

50. *A tallit* (prayer shawl)

51. A fringed garment worn underneath one's clothes all day

52. A white linen garment bound by a white belt worn at the temple for high holidays, at Pesach, by a groom and as a shroud.

53. *Shulchan Aruch* (*The Ready Table*)

54. An electric razor and scissors are permitted.

55. *Haggadah*

56. Hanukah

57. Purim

58. It is symbolically sold. A bit is burned in a ceremonial manner.

59. 49

60. Ten

61. *"Chad Gaddiah"*

62. Passover

63. They are set from right to left.

64. They are lit from left to right.

65. The fast of the first-born son

66. Manna and quail

67. An *etrog*

68. The *peetom*

69. Tu b'Shevat

70. Eight

71. Yom Kippur

72. *Sh'lach manot*

73. The days of the Omer

74. Matzoh

75. Its production is closely monitored from harvest to baking.

76. The mention of the name of Haman

77. Tishrei (Rosh Hashanna, Yom Kippur, Sukkot)

78. Sukkot, Passover and Shavuot

79. The singing of *zemirot* (songs and hymns)

80. Observance of a commandment, or a good deed

81. Carp, whitefish and pike

82. *Lulav* and *etrog*

83. Rosh Hashanna

84. The coming of a sweet New Year

85. Simchat Torah

86. Myrtle and willow

87. The new month on the new moon

88. A fringe usually on the corner of a tallit

89. Shemini Atzeret

90. They are recited in one breath.

91. The youngest at the table

92. The shield of David, referred to as the star of David

93. *Shaddai* (G-d)

94. Denotes the number of *mitzvot* in the Bible

95. Gimmel wins the pot, Shin antes into the pot, Hay wins half the pot, and Nunn wins nothing.

96. Hanukah

97. The *shamas*

98. A *menorah* has spaces for any number of candles. A *hanukiah* is a Hanukah *menorah* with spaces for nine candles.

99. Wool and flax

100. The mortar which the slaves used in Egypt

101. The new moon

102. Shavuot

103. Inward

104. 33

105. The Prophet Elijah

106. Shabbat

107. Waive the *lulav* and *etrog* together, eat and sleep

108. Order

109. Ten

110. Havdalah candle, spice and wine

111. At the Seder, children are encouraged to steal the Afikomen (or hidden matzoh).

112. Purim

113. *Mechitzah*

114. *Matzoh*

115. By placing two challahs at the Shabbat table

116. Ten

117. As each is mentioned, a drop of wine is spilled.

118. Blood, frogs, vermin, beasts, cattle disease, boils, hail, locusts, darkness, and slaying of the first born

119. *Shema*

120. Aramaic

121. The *Alenu* prayer on Rosh Hashanna and Yom Kippur

122. Sins

123. Simhat Torah

124. The appearance of the first three stars in the heavens

125. Shank bone, bitter herbs, charoset, parsley and an egg which has been burned

126. A. Hanukah, B. Shavuot, C. Purim

127. A. Sukkot, B. Shavuot, C. Hanukah, D. Purim

128. Tisha b'Av

129. *"L'Cha Dodi"*

130. Hanukah

131. Hello, goodbye and peace

CREATIVE ARTS

1. Leon Uris

2. *My Name Is Asher Lev*

3. *Blood Accusation*

4. Norman Podhoretz

5. Hephzibah plays the piano.

6. Lawrence, Massachusetts

7. Pablo Casals

8. Sholom Secunda

9. Allen Ginsberg

10. Victor David Brenner

11. Ceiling of the Sistene Chapel, Rome

12. Rembrandt van Rijn

13. *Guns of August*

14. *Der Tag, Morning Journal, Daily Forward,* and *Freiheit*

15. *The Forward*

16. Isaac Leib Peretz

17. *East of Eden*

18. *The Jewish Catalog* and *The Second Jewish Catalog and Yellow Pages*

19. Solomon Bloomgarden

20. Martin Buber

21. *Mayor*

22. Gertrude Stein

23. Saul Bellow

24. Leo Rosten

25. Amsterdam (1686)

26. *Judenstaat*

27. Gertrude Stein

28. Pinky Pearl

29. Sholomo Carlebach

30. *The Fixer*

31. Mendele Mocher Sephorim

32. (a) "*Hatikvah*" (b) "The Hope"

33. Naftali Herz Imber

34. Abraham Cahan

35. Jacob Adler

36. David Pinski

37. A ball-point pen

38. Klezmer

39. Bel Kaufman

40. Curtis Institute for Music, Philadelphia

41. He is an actor.

42. The Andrew Sisters

43. *Jerusalem Post*

44. *Call It Sleep*

45. Joan Comay

46. A man who travels from country to country in search of the Messiah

47. A cobbler who taunted Jesus and therefore is condemned to have no home

48. *The Rise of David Levinksy*

49. Abraham Cahan

50. Moses, Raphael and Isaac; Moses and Raphael are twins.

51. Bashka Paeff of Cambridge, Massachusetts

52. Marc Chagall

53. *Goodbye Columbus.* Richard Benjamin was the male lead.

54. Abraham Mapu

55. *Daniel Deronda*

56. *Trial and Error*

57. Violin

58. Sholem Asch

59. "Oyfn Pripetchik"

60. George Gershwin

61. *Rabbi Elimeylekh*

62. Abraham Joshua Heschel (1907-1972)

63. *A Bintel Brief*, addressed to Abraham Cahan

64. The 12 Tribes of Israel

65. Pissarro

66. Sir Jacob Epstein

67. Amadeo Modigliani

68. Isaac Stern

69. Irving Berlin

70. Edna Ferber (1887-1968); *So Big*

71. I.J.

72. Bennett Alfred Cerf

73. They were Hazzanim. the talented Koussevitsky brothers.

74. "White Christmas", written by Irving Berlin

75. Ben Shahn (1898-1969)

76. Hayyim N. Bialik

77. *Rozhinkes Mit Mandlen*

78. Joseph (Yossele) Rosenblatt

79. Leonard Bernstein

80. Aaron Copland

81. "Jerusalem of Gold"

82. They are professional singers.

83. Sigmund Romberg

84. Cantor-actor

85. Ernest Bloch (1880-1959)

86. The first woman before Eve, supposedly a demon

87. Felix was Moses' grandson.

88. President John F. Kennedy

89. Chaim Potok

90. Tsimble (dulcimer-like), viol (fiddle family) and baraban (drums)

91. The fiddle

92. Franz Kafka

93. *Herzog*

94. The pianist Vladimir Horowitz

95. 1. d
    2. c
    3. f
    4. a
    5. e
    6. b

96 Jubal

97. Helena Rubinstein

98. Roman Vishniac

99. They were all cantors.

100. Erica Jong

101. Purim Shpiel (play at Purim)

102. Richard Tucker and Jan Peerce were brothers-in-law.

103. The Joseph H. Hirshhorn Museum of Art and Sculpture Garden of the Smithsonian

104. Billy Rose

105. Isaac Asimov

106. *Humbolt's Gift*

107. "Bubbles"

108. George S. Kaufman

109.   Joe Rosenthal

110.   Benny Goodman

111.   Carly Simon

112.   Jacques Offenbach

113.   Theodor Herzl

114.   *The Source*

115.   *Death of a Salesman*

116.   Dustin Hoffman

117.   Herb Alpert

118.   Rebecca Gratz of Philadelphia, who founded the first Hebrew School

119.   Jerome David Salinger

120.   The *horah*

121.   Honi-Ha-Meaggel is said to have slept for 70 years.

122.   Irving Stone

123.   Burt Bacharach

124.   Marvin Hamlich

125.   Marilyn and Alan Bergman

126.   Jascha Heifetz

127.   Al Capp

128.   Harry Golden

129. Theodore H. White

130. (a) Bloch Publishing Co.
(b) Edward Block and Rabbi Isaac Mayer Wise

131. Lillian Hellman

132. Maurice Sendak

133. Herman Wouk

134. Marc Chagall

135. Dankmar Adler

136. Leopold Bloom

137. John Rubinstein

138. Hanna Green

139. The Guggenheim Museum of Modern Art

140. Efrem Zimbalist Sr.

141.

1. c	8. a
2. f	9. b
3. h	10. d
4. m	11. l
5. g	12. i
6. j	13. e
7. k	

GEOGRAPHY

1. b

2. U.S., Israel, USSR and France

3. Ben-Gurion Airport

4. Waltham, Massachusetts

5. David Steinman

6. Louisville, Kentucky

7. War of 1967 (Six Day War)

8. First mayor of Tel-Aviv

9. All communities outside of Israel

10. The synagogue

11. Hester Street

12. Mount Ararat

13. Bethlehem

14. Nazareth

15. It is located at a point below sea level lower than any other settlement on earth.

16. Mt. Carmel

17. Masada

18. The Dead Sea is 1,296 feet below sea level.

19. The Dead Sea Scrolls

20. Kaifeng

21. Entebbe, Uganda

22. c

23. Hughenden Manor (High Wycombe England)

24. On Mt. Meron (3,963 ft)

25. Milk and honey

26. S'deh Boker

27. Harbor defense post until 1890

28. The Arabs

29. Crown Heights, Brooklyn, NYC

30. Eilat

31. Galilee

32. Waddeston Manor, Aylesbury England

33. Denver, Colorado

34. India

35. Vincennes, Indiana

36. Merkavia

37. Damascus, Jaffa, Zion, Lions, Dung, Herod's, Mercy and New

38. Mercy Gate is closed until the Messiah arrives.

39. Mea She'arim

40. Mediterranean and Red Seas

41. Mt. Scopus

42. Germany

43. Dunedin, New Zealand

44. 650,000

45. Three million

46. The Dead Sea Scrolls

47. The Ritz

48. Yonah Schimmel's

49. The Uriah Levy family

50. Yeshiva University

51. It was the home of Albert Einstein.

52. It is the site where Abraham brought Isaac to be sacrificed to God.

53. The lower course of the western wall surrounding Herod's Temple

54. Daniel Sieff Research Center

55. Baghdad, Iraq

56. At the foot of the Mount of Olives, outside Jerusalem

57. Goshen

58. Marco Polo

59. "Operation Magic Carpet"

60. Turkey

61. 500,000

62. Rishon Le-Zion

63. King Solomon

64. The Mount of Olives

65. The Borscht Belt

66. Grossingers

67. Lebanon, Syria, Jordan and Egypt

68. c

69. Mediterranean, Red and Dead Seas, Kinneret and Hula

70. Florence, Italy

71. 127 miles

72. NYC, Los Angeles, Philadelphia, Chicago and Miami

73. The Yarkon

74. Approx. 84%

75. Three million

76. Prague, Czechoslovakia (12th century)

77. Charleston, South Carolina

78. Chatham Square, NYC

79. Tanglewood

80. On Wall Street in NYC (New Amsterdam, 1660)

81. Kiev, Russia

82. Mecca, Saudi Arabia

83. Milwaukee, Wisconsin

84. Lake Kinneret

85. Red Sea

86. Rabbat Ammon

87. 1909

88. Shalom Tower; 460 feet high

89. Tel Aviv University

90. The Red Sea (two branches)

91. 400-2559

92. Jacksonville (1850)

93. Gaza

94. Jordan

95. Jaffa

96. Philadelphia, PA

97. Modin

98. Nazareth

99. Fifth Avenue and 92 Street

100. Ramat Gan, Israel

101. Amsterdam, Holland

102. Syria

103. On the road from Jerusalem to Bethlehem

104. Chelm

PICTURE THIS

Answers to Pictures

Picture — Page 101

1. Outside the Parliament building (Knesset) in Jerusalem.

2. a) The British Parliament
   b) The Israeli Parliament

Pictures — Page 102

1. A

2. *Chai*

Picture — Page 103

1. Haifa

2. The Baha'i Shrine

3. David Ben-Gurion Boulevard

Picture — Page 104

1. When the eighth night of Hanukah falls on Shabbat.

2. The Hanukah candles. (One should not light anything during Shabbat.)

Picture — Page 105

1. The Wailing Wall and the Western Wall

2. Herod's Temple, Solomon's Temple, and the Second Temple

3. The Mosque of Omar

Picture — Page 106

1. *Shabbat*

2. Challah

3. Yom Kippur and Passover

Picture — Page 107

1. Touro Synagogue

2. Newport, Rhode Island

3. It's the oldest synagogue in the United States still in use.

Picture — Page 108

1. *Dreidlach*

2. *S'vivonim*

3. Hanukah

Picture — Page 109

1. Citadel of Masada

2. King Herod

3. The Zealots of Masada

4. Eleazar ben Jair

Picture — Page 110

1. The Ten Commandments

2. They rise.

Picture — Page 111

1. Justice Louis D. Brandeis

2. Brandeis University, Waltham, Massachusetts

Picture — Page 112

1. Jerusalem

2. The wall of the Old City of Jerusalem

3. Mount of Olives

Picture — Page 113

1. David Ben-Gurion

2. Chaim Weizmann

3. David Ben-Gurion

Picture — Page 114

1. North of Elat, Israel

2. King Solomon

3. Copper mines

Picture — Page 115

1. Hurva Synagogue

2. The Old City of Jerusalem

3. 19th (1856)

4. Jordanians

Picture — Page 116

1. Hayyim Nachman Bialik

2. Hebrew poetry

3. Tel Aviv

Picture — Page 117

1. Bet She'arim, Israel

2. 2nd century

3. The Romans

Picture — Page 118

1. The Phasael Tower

2. Herod

3. In the Old City of Jerusalem

Picture — Page 119

1. Tel Aviv

2. The Mediterranean Sea

3. The Dan Hotel, Astor Hotel, Sheraton Hotel, Ramada Continental and the Plaza

Picture — Page 120

1. *The Jewish Bride*

2. The Rijksmuseum, Amsterdam

3. Rembrandt van Rijn

Pictures — Page 121

1. Henry Wadsworth Longfellow

2. *The Jewish Cemetery In Newport*

3. 1677

4. Abraham Touro, Moses Seixas, Aaron Lopez, Jacob Rivera and Judah Touro (Abraham's brother)

5. Jacob Rivera

AND MORE

1. She is the first female Conservative rabbi.

2. August Von Wasserman

3. Paul Ehrlich

4. Carl Sagan

5. Niels Bohr

6. Bernard Baruch

7. Franz Boas

8. Isaac Jacobi

9. George Wald

10. Doar Ivri (Hebrew Post)

11. Two coins issued by Bar-Kochba

12. The influence of x-rays in genetics

13. Albert Sabin

14. Solomon Schecter

15. Albert Michelson

16. Alan M. Dershowitz

17. Sigmund Freud

18. "Ma-Oz-Tzur"

19. By adding one month

20. "Good Day" or "Happy Holiday"

21. Rube Goldberg

22. Emma Goldman

23. Newport, Rhode Island

24. Dublin, Ireland

25. Twenty cents

26. "Dr. Ruth" Westheimer

27. Borscht is made from beets.

28. Adar Bet (Sheni)

29. *World of Our Fathers*

30. Roger William Straus. His grand-father was Oscar Solomon Straus.

31. Filene's

32. Landsmannschaft

33. *Imma* and *abba*

34. "Ani-Ma-Amin (I Believe)"

35. Sarah Bernhardt

36. Bat Mitzvah

37. Shekel

38. *Tallit* (prayer shawl)

39. Emma Lazarus

40. "Shabbat Sholom"

41. Shubert Alley

42. c

43. JFK, New York

44. Morris Fishbein

45. Ultra-orthodox Yeshiva students, women from ultra orthodox homes and married women

46. Seagram, Ltd.

47. Seven

48. a) Harry F., b) Daniel, c) Solomon

49. Moshe Safdie

50. "Aleichem Shalom"